My Life An Open Book

Valencia Black

DEDICATION

This book is dedicated to Hubert Carl Black. He was a good husband who helped me in every way that he could.

CONTENTS

PREFACE

I learned that every harsh condition, every catastrophe, every mental anguish brings with it the foundation of matching or Hugh blessing in God.

For five years I carried a burden that was simply too heavy for me to bear, a burden that caused me to hide in the shadow of my yesterday. Guilt, depression, shame, disappointment, loneliness, anger, fear and a broken heart gripped me and held me within my internal hallways of darkness, wondering every day what would happen next. Once outgoing, fun-loving, playful and enjoying life, I saw my life change in the twinkling of an eye. Everything that I once thought to be the truth became a lie.

I had always dreamed of having children of my own. I used to dream of how many children I wanted, what they would look like and what kind of mother I would be. I always dreamed of having a loving family, living in a beautiful home and being happy. After marrying the love of my life, we found out that we could not conceive of a child of our own. God was trying to tell me something. However, that burning desire to have a family never subsided, and with my husband's agreement I decided to adopt children and make them my own. That decision changed the course of my life and sent me on the road to learning what true love and forgiveness is.

One Sunday morning my world was turned upside down. I used to wonder how a mother could wake up one day and decide to leave her family, her children, her home, everything that was near and dear to her heart and not look back. I wondered what it would take for a woman to do that. Should I leave? Should I stay? Those were the questions that were running rampantly through my mind, 24 hours a day for seven years.

Guilt ravaged my heart and my mind on a daily basis. Was it my fault? Did I miss the signs? I was convinced it was my fault. If I had only listened to God, my family would not be in this predicament. If I had only heeded the voice that I could hear speaking within me since I was a child. I would not be in the place that I am now. God told me not to adopt my children, especially my girls. He told me not to do it. But I was determined to have my own way. I was determined to have a family no matter what. I wanted children of my own. Since I could not have them, I decided that I would take care of children that other people did not want and make them my own.

What do you do when the very person that you never thought would hurt you suddenly turns? What do you do when the vows that you pledge are challenged and you find yourself at the crossroads of whether to break them or keep them? What happens when you put your husband in the place of Christ? No one should be able to take the place of Christ - no one.

I am a living demonstration of what God can do. From 1991, my life has not been easy. I have had to deal with one of the most revolting, disappointing and shameful situations that life could throw my way. My husband had committed an act that I did not know was even humanly possible for him to commit. He violated an area of trust that on the surface was beyond repair.

"For if you forgive men when they sin against you, your heavenly Father will also forgive you. But if you do not forgive men their sins, your Father will not forgive your sins." (Matthew 6:14-15)

"In sickness and in health…" I promised to love him in sickness and in health. Did "health" only mean physical health? He violated my trust and the trust of our children. He sexually molested our young daughters in our home. He hurt the very thing that was near and dear to my heart, the thing that I prayed for. However, God did tell me not to bring children into our home. He also told me to get the children out of our home and do not adopt them. I did not listen to God. I wanted what I wanted and I did what I wanted. Now, what? I asked myself, "What do I do now? Do I leave him or do I stay? Do I forgive him and move on with our lives, or do I walk out, shut the door and never look back? For after all, I did not obey God. I opened the door wide and allowed the sleeping evil within my husband to awaken.

I loved my family more than anything in the world. I did not want to see my family torn apart. I did not want to lose my children. I wanted to be able to forgive my husband and help him heal and be made whole.

In order to move forward you have to keep your eyes on Christ. You have to keep your eyes on your future. You have to keep your eyes on His word. Yes, it hurts. Yes, there will be tears. Yes, you will feel like your heart is being ripped out of your chest. But if God can raise the dead, isn't God great enough that he can raise the living? If God can forgive us of our sins, aren't we, as His children who were made in His image, able forgive our brothers and sisters?

My heart was broken. My trust was broken. My spirit was broken. But I know a God who can fix everything. I know a God who can heal, set free and deliver. I know a God who is bigger than any problem. I had to forget those things that were behind me and make a conscious decision to move forward. My hurt, my pain, my love, my journey to reclaim what God has for me… this is My Story.

"Greater love hath no man than this that a man lay down his life for his friends." (John 15:13)

CHAPTER 1

THE PERFECT START

We Received Christ

Hubert and I lived together for five years. He took very good care of me. He helped pay rent and other bills. He drove me or allowed me to drive his car anywhere I wanted to go. When I worked nights, he picked me up, and he took my coworkers home simply because I asked without complaining.

During those five years, God began to move in our lives. We began to watch religious programs on television, which sparked our curiosity about God, Jesus, and Bible prophecy. Once we started watching the religious programs, we noticed that in public places, like the mall, young adults around our age would approach us with gospel tracks and a few tried to witness to us. Through the religious programs, tracks and witnessing, the Holy Spirit prepared our minds to receive the gospel message and Jesus Christ as our Savior and Lord.

Our Journey Towards Christ

After several months of watching Christian programs, I heard the gospel and received Jesus Christ as my Lord and Savior. Immediately, God encouraged me to attend church. I attended a local church that was three blocks away from our apartment. A couple of weeks later while watching Christian television, Hubert received Jesus Christ as Savior and Lord as well. After we accepted Jesus as our savior, God encouraged us to get married. We were married about a month later.

We attended a mega church as a couple for five years. The pastor pronounced a prophetic word over our lives around the third Sunday of our attendance. I thought this prophetic word was a looming curse.

The Haunting Prophetic Word

It was a normal Sunday morning. Hubert and I attended a service. We were sitting in the main sanctuary when a prophetic word came from the pastor. He said there was a couple there who needed to come up so that he could minister to them. Hubert and I were sitting a few rows from the where the pastor was standing. He made the call two or three times without making any indication to whom he was talking. He just stood there and repeated that there was a couple that needed to come to the altar. No one moved. I felt like he was talking to us, but I did not move and I did not say anything to Hubert. I was afraid. I didn't want to stand up in front of the entire congregation. Finally, after no response, the pastor stated that since the two people did not get up, they were going to experience some kind of terrible heartbreak.

After the service, Hubert and I looked at each other and agreed that we thought the pastor was talking about us. We looked up and the pastor was still at the front of the church. I thought about approaching him as he was talking to a few people who were around him. As I continued to think about it, he began walking out of the sanctuary. It was too late. We did not take heed to God's voice. I was 22, and Hubert was 25.

Over the next 10 years, I thought about the prophecy often. Periodically, I would examine my life to see if we were doing anything to cause the prophecy come to pass. Eight years passed and we were safe. Then I persuaded Hubert to become a foster parent, and we started down the path to terrible heartbreak. We had set our course to fulfilling the prophetic word in more ways than one.

CHAPTER 2

THE VOICE ECHOING FROM WITHIN

Still Dreaming…

Hubert and I married after five years of living together. During the early years of our relationship, I did not get pregnant. I was fine with this at the time because I was in school and children were not a priority. However, after we were married, children became a priority for me. There were times when I questioned the fact that I was not using any form of birth control and did not get pregnant, but I was not too concerned. I thought that when I wanted to get pregnant, I would focus on it and it would happen, because after all, I was young, saved and married. We followed the Bible teachings of our pastor who gave us instruction on how to prepare for a family. I was taught that God would give me anything that was in line with His word and His will. I was taught that His word was His will. All I had to do was believe and receive by faith. I was married, saved and serving the Lord with all of my heart. We purchased a home in a nice neighborhood, but year after year passed, and I did not get pregnant.

After three to four years of watching our friends, family and neighbors having children, I became very concerned about not getting pregnant. I decided to seek medical intervention and began my first round of fertility treatments. My first gynecologist began the process and referred me to several specialists in his network. One of the tests was extremely painful for me. The doctor injected dye into my fallopian tubes, which was so painful that I began calling on the name of Jesus. The test was negative. My fallopian tubes were open. The other tests for me were negative as well.

My doctor then referred us to a specialist at a major university. Hubert needed to be tested. We saw the specialist and underwent several tests. The results revealed that Hubert had a low sperm count, and they prescribed a treatment to help us. They took Hubert's sperm, spun it down and placed it into my cervical area. We underwent this procedure a number of times, but still no pregnancy. I was 26 and Hubert was 29 when we were told that the last procedure was negative - no pregnancy. We went home and I cried in Hubert's arms, as we laid in bed talking about the results. I had almost resigned in my mind that we were going to be childless. But I still had a glimmer of hope because I believed in God.

I was taught every week about faith in church and bible study. I decided to discontinue the fertility treatments. I believed that God would bless us in a supernatural way. Another two years passed and still no pregnancy. My neighbor suggested foster parenting to us. Several of the older women on our block were foster parents and I thought it would be a good alternative for us. However, the more I pondered the thought, I felt a very bad feeling deep inside of me. I ignored the warning of the Lord. I desperately wanted children in my life. I encouraged Hubert to become a foster parent with me. In retrospect, I felt like Eve encouraging Adam to eat the forbidden fruit knowing that neither one of us should be eating it.

Ignoring the voice of God within me, I decided to move forward with us becoming foster parents. We completed the process and were assigned our first child. She was a sweet little girl with very short hair. Her hair was damaged due to lack of care in her previous placement. She stayed with us for two months and was later adopted by a single businesswoman.

Subsequently, we had four short placements in our first home. God warned me several times not to continue accepting children, but again, I ignored the warnings because everything seemed to be going well. I took care of the children. Hubert worked nights, and I made sure that the children did not disturb him during the day. On his days off, we were out and about and Hubert visited with his friends or family.

After four years in our first home, we began to have trouble with the next-door neighbor. Her long-term foster children were teenagers. Her foster son was involved in gangs. A bullet that was meant for him came through our front window. We decided that it was time to move. We moved to a bigger house. Our neighbors did not have school-aged children. In our new home, we decided to make one last attempt at having natural children.

The Final Attempt

Fertility technology has come a long way over the years. Women much older than me were having children through a process called invitro fertilization. I saw a program on television about older women in their 40s and 50s conceiving children. At the time I was only 33 years-old. I thought, if they can conceive a child this way, maybe I can too.

Hubert and I celebrate our birthdays in the same month. Weeks before our birthdays, we began another series of fertility testing. The initial tests were the same type as before, but with an important second step - fertilization in a petri dish. After completion and analysis of the tests, I was given medication to inject daily for several weeks. I was able to accomplish the daily injections with Hubert's help. The next steps involved harvesting the eggs from my ovaries and the fertilization process. Both procedures were a success. The doctors gave us a picture of the fertilized eggs. As I looked at the picture, I began to feel that uneasy feeling again. I heard the inner voice saying, "No, do not spend any money on the procedure," but I ignored the voice and the feeling.

Finally, the time came to place the eggs into my uterus. The office staff reviewed the fees for the procedure with us. The cost was $5,000. I heard the voice within me say, *"Do not pay for it."* I ignored the voice and paid for the procedure anyway. I wanted it to work with all of my heart. Immediately after I paid, the doctors performed the procedure. When I arrived home, I looked at the picture of the fertilized eggs. I was building up my enthusiasm when I heard the voice again, just as clear as Hubert talking to me, say, *"It is not going to work."*

I stood there looking at the picture saying aloud, *"Why?"* I did not get a response. I sat down on the bed holding the picture in my hand wondering what was wrong with me. Why couldn't I be blessed? What horrible sin had I committed that God would speak to me in an audible voice and tell me, no? As I looked over my life, I could not pinpoint a sin that I felt was so horrible that I deserved this type of severe punishment. I put the picture on the headboard and quietly sat in the room alone for two hours.

A few days later, I took a pregnancy test. When the results were ready the doctor called us in for a meeting. There was a counselor in the meeting with us. He began saying that we were the youngest of the four couples that they were working with at that time. The three other couples were each over 40. One couple's odds were extremely low. He informed us that that each of the couples conceived, but we did not. The doctor was completely puzzled by our results. He said the procedure should have worked for us. Then he looked at me. He was surprised by my emotional response. I did not cry. I was not upset. I just sat there and listened to him tell us what I already knew. That was our final visit to the fertility clinic and my final attempt to get pregnant using medical means. I assumed that I was cursed by God for some unknown reason and that was the end of that.

Moving Forward

After my decision to cease my attempts to conceive, I decided that I wanted to take care of foster babies because I wanted to eventually adopt a child. Within a few days of this decision and for one year following, all we were assigned were infant and toddler placements. As the year came to an end, I felt the need to stop foster care and begin the process to adopt. However, I had accepted a foster placement of two little girls, one, four years-old and one, 18 months.

I was very careful when deciding whether or not to adopt the girls. Both girls had been in long term foster placement before coming to our home, and they had bonded with the foster parents. I did not want us to be another broken parental bond in their lives, so I considered adopting them.

When the social worker who placed children in our home came for a monthly visit, I told her that we wanted to adopt a baby boy. She asked me about the two girls, and I told her that we were thinking about adopting them, but we had not made the final decision. She began searching for a baby boy to place in our home for adoption. A few weeks later, we received a three-day-old baby boy. After two months of taking care of him, I asked my husband if we could adopt him. He agreed. I called the social worker and told her that we wanted to adopt him. She asked me about the girls. I told her that I would have to call her back because we had not decided yet. I asked Hubert if we could adopt all three children. He said if that was what I wanted to do that it was all right with him.

I felt the release from God to adopt the boy, but when it came to adopting the girls that same feeling of dread would overtake me. It was almost as if I could feel God saying, no. It was not an audible sound, but the deep, intense feeling that you get when you know you have done something wrong and your parents are coming to get you or you have been discovered doing something that they told you not to do. Whenever I would think about it, that intense dread would come over me, and I would sit back and think why. Then I would dismiss it.

There were times that I wanted to give into the voice within me telling me to only adopt my son, but then I would feel regret. These two beautiful little girls had been with me for such a long time, and now I was going to let them go and just keep my son. I could not allow myself to do that. Although I had the constant feeling of dread, I would look at them and think, *"They have already been through so much. Why would I want to add to their pain?"* Not knowing that I was about to add something that was going to be far worse than anything they had gone through before. There was no doubt in my mind that God was saying, no.

Even though I kept having the intense feeling of dread about adopting the children, I did not see a problem with adopting. I wanted children in my life. I believed that Hubert also wanted to adopt the children or he would have told me no. We were good parents. Our home would be a great place for a child needing a permanent home. Nevertheless, I did not rush the adoption process. We waited nearly a year before moving forward with the adoptions.

Before we went to the court to finalize and sign the final adoption papers, once again that intense feeling of dread came over my whole body. For hours I sat thinking about not going through with the adoption process. I decided to move forward with the process. I looked at the children who were calling me mommy. We had bonded. I did not want to give them up. I ignored the feeling, and we moved forward with the process.

Weeks after signing the final papers, I experienced the same intense feeling of dread. I thought, *"God told me not to do this. It's not too late. I can call the agency and let them know that I've changed my mind."* Many days I sat in my living room wondering why I felt such hesitation, but I did not receive an answer to my question. I believe that God wanted me to trust and obey Him. However, I continued to ignore the feeling. I did not give the children back. We adopted them, and I attempted to move forward with our lives

In time, the feelings of dread went away and our lives were normal. We were still foster parents, so we continued to accept short term placements. One spring day, I received a telephone call and was asked to take my two sisters. One was eight, and the other was five, the same age as our oldest daughter. I accepted the placement. The social worker brought the girls over and introduced them to me and our two daughters. They were beautiful little girls. After the social worker left, I gave the girls a tour of the house and introduced them to my son. He was in his crib asleep, but he woke up when we came into the room talking. Next, I showed them their room.

Later in the day, Hubert woke up and I introduced them to him. The sisters heard our daughters calling us mommy and daddy, and they wanted to know if they could refer to us in the same way. I reminded them that they already had a mother and father, but if they wanted to call us mommy and daddy, that was all right with us. The girls lived with us for five years.

From time to time, I would get a check in my spirit that I made the wrong decision. But again, I would ignore it because I trusted my husband. I never imagined that he would do anything to hurt me or our children, so I did not see a problem. I wanted what I wanted. I was determined to have my own way. Ultimately, I had my own way and I paid the cost for it - not only me, but my entire family.

CHAPTER 3

THE PAIN OF DISCOVERY

And it Came to Pass...

It was five years after adopting our three children and accepting two foster daughters that I began to see the troubling prophetic word that we received at our church begin to unfold in our lives. It was early one Sunday morning, around 1:00 a.m. I awakened suddenly and missed my husband lying next to me. I immediately got out of my bed and began to look for him. I checked in the den, but He was not there. I came back through the kitchen and walked through the dining room into the hallway. I still did not find him. I checked my son's room and the middle bedroom where my other two daughters slept, but he was not there. I approached the front bedroom where my youngest daughter and oldest daughter slept. I looked in and my youngest daughter was in bed. However, when I looked at the top bunk bed, my oldest daughter was not there. I turned and looked at the bathroom door and I did not see a light from the bottom of the door.

Slowly, I looked at the garage door. It was the only place that I had not checked. I walked to the door, opened it and witnessed the tragic scenario that would ultimately change the course of our lives. I stood there in the open door and watched my husband with our daughter. He was not on top of her, but he was doing something to her. I could not see what he was doing because he was standing in front of her and his back was to me. I was overwhelmed with shock, disappointment, sadness and fear. My husband was molesting our daughter. When he heard the garage door open, he stopped and my daughter ran to me.

My daughter and I went to my bedroom and sat on the side of my bed, waiting for him to come into the room. She was crying uncontrollably and saying, *"I'm sorry."* I took her in my arms and held her close, as I whispered in her ear over and over again, *"It is not your fault."* She was only a child. Two minutes later, my husband came into the room. I told him to shut the door. I did not want to awaken our other children.

I was crying a little as I sat there holding our daughter and looking at my husband. I felt something deep within me as he talked to me. I was angry, shocked and hurt, but I was not out of control. I felt a little dizzy and lightheaded, but I was able to shake off that feeling. Then the prophetic word replayed in my mind. Suddenly, I felt a kick in my stomach. I wanted to cry hysterically, but I could not because I was holding my daughter and I did not want to hurt her any more than she was already hurting. My daughter felt that the incident was her fault. I did not want my emotions to add to her feelings of guilt, so I kept my emotions under control. I spoke to my husband in a low voice. I said, *"The prophecy that our first pastor spoke to us has come to pass."*

Hubert stood there looking at me as he cried. I felt like my life had just come to an end and I was not prepared to die. In between the tears I said, *"I trusted you. I never thought that you would hurt me or our child in this way."* My thoughts were going a mile a minute. I had a child for whom I needed to get help, a husband that needed help, and I had other children in the house that he may have molested. Shaking my head, I walked with my daughter back to her room.

I went back to our bedroom and continued to interrogate my husband. I needed to know if he penetrated our daughter. He swore that he did not penetrate her. I hoped that he was telling me the truth, but I did not take his word alone. I went back to my daughter, took her into another room and asked her privately if my husband hurt her with his penis. She said, no. I believed her because I did not see any blood or bodily fluids on her; I did not see any blood in her underwear; and she did not complain about pain in her vaginal area. I walked my daughter back to her room.

My youngest daughter was awakened by the noise. I told my daughters to go take a bath and get ready for church, as I laid out their church clothes - dresses, underwear, and stockings. My other two daughters had awakened, and I told them to start getting ready for church as well. They knew something was wrong, so they asked me. I told them that we would talk about it after church. I went into my son's bedroom, woke him up, took him into the bathroom and got him ready for church. I gave him a bowl of cereal to eat while I checked on my daughters' progress. Only two of my four daughters had to bathe, because the other two had bathed the night before. My oldest daughter had to bathe because of what Hubert had done to her, and my youngest daughter had to bathe because she had wet the bed. I thought to myself, I should have recognized the bedwetting as a sign.

My youngest daughter had stopped wetting the bed before this incident, then she began wetting the bed again. I asked her what was wrong, but she did not tell me. I thought she was just going through another bedwetting phase because she was drinking too much before bed or I was giving her too many sweets.

I tried to keep moving along as if nothing had happened. When everyone was dressed, I drove the children to church. Hubert remained at home. I did not want him in the car with us.

If I Had Only Listened

When we arrived at church my children went to their respective Sunday school classes and I went to the main sanctuary. When my pastor began speaking, he immediately changed his normal routine. He said, *"God wants to minister to a woman. She is not a younger woman, but she is not older either."* At the time, I was 37 years-old. He said, *"You have placed your husband in the position of Christ. No man belongs in that position."* He was right. I believed that my husband would never hurt me. The pastor laid his hands on my forehead. I received the power of God and I went back to my seat.

After church we went home. I sat down and thought about what happened and what I should do next. I thought that the devil had the nerve to walk into my house and attack our children by using my husband. I thought about what I would do if a stranger had come into our home and attacked my children. I would fight the intruder and with God's help and win. I thought, if God could raise the dead, if God raised Lazarus who was dead for days, his body decomposing and stinking badly, God can surely raise the living dead. If God could raise the stinking, decomposing dead and give them life, then God can help the stinking, decomposing body and mind of the living dead. I believed that God had the power to change Hubert (if he wanted to be changed), and to heal our family.

I thought, *"I am not going down like this. The devil will not win. If Hubert were willing to do whatever he needed to do to change, then it's on!"* I prayed to God and repented. I thought, *"If I had listened to God, I would not be in this situation. But now is not the time for me to wallow in self-pity. I need to fight and win."* I asked the Lord to help me fight and to save my family.

I stood up from the place that I was sitting, and I felt this intense pain in the center of my chest. I placed my right hand on my chest. The pain seemed like it was coming from my physical heart, but I knew it was not physical. I knew that I would have to live with this heartache and cope with the pain. As I walked into another room the pain diminished until it was totally gone. I stopped walking, lowered my head, closed my eyes, and thanked God for taking the pain away.

The next day I told my girls to meet me in the living room. Hubert was at work and my son was in his room playing with his toys. I asked each daughter if Hubert had touched them in their private area in anyway. My oldest daughter said that he did not touch her, but my three youngest daughters each said that he had touched them. I sent them to their rooms.

I brought my son into the living room and sat him on the couch next to me. He was four years-old. I held his hand and I asked him if his father touched him in his private area in any way. He said, no. I asked him again using one of my daughter's Barbie dolls that he had stripped and tore off the head. I pointed to the spot in the middle of her legs and I asked him again had his daddy touched him in between his

19

legs. I had my finger resting on the private area of the doll. He said, no. I was reasonably satisfied with my son's response. I bathed and dressed my son every day, and I would have noticed any unusual swelling, bleeding or marks on him. My daughters were old enough to bathe themselves.

When I finished talking to our son, I left him in the living room watching television. I went into our bedroom and I packed my husband's clothes. He was at work when I questioned the children. He arrived home two hours later, at his usual time, between 8:30 and 9:30 a.m. He saw his suitcases packed. I was sitting in the recliner on the side of the bed. He did not say anything until I said, *"I talked with the girls and our son and each one of them, except the oldest girl and our son said you touched them."* He said he did not. I told him that I did not believe him; I believed them. He started to cry.

I told him that he could tell me the truth. I was strong enough to take it. Then he admitted that he had touched them. Immediately, I told him that he had to leave. I picked up the telephone and offered it to him. I said, *"Call your mother and tell her that you need to move back in with her."* He cried, *"No, no!"* He would not take the telephone. I hung up the telephone and said, *"Do you want to call one of your brothers?"* He declined. *"Then what do you want to do?"* He sat crying, holding his head down. After a few moments of silence he responded, *"I will find an apartment."* I quickly agreed.

He took a shower and immediately went out looking for an apartment. There was a new multi-unit apartment complex that was just built near his job. He went there and rented a furnished one-bedroom apartment. He came back to the house, put his suitcases in the car and left.

I Never Saw It Coming

Before we accepted foster children into our home Hubert had joy about him. He had this big, beautiful smile that disappeared after a few years, along with his cheerful attitude. A few years after we became foster parents Hubert's demeanor began to change. The change was slow and subtle. Each year he became less interested in going out together or visiting our parents together. He stopped going out with his friends. He complained of being too tired. I accepted his word because his hours had increased at work for a few years. However, by the fifth year, I noticed a major difference in his attitude. The anti-social behavior had gotten worse. He did not want to be around friends and relatives.

All I could do was pray. I would walk around the house and pray. In those days, I prayed a lot (two plus hours per day). The children and I would have prayer and praise in the den on Saturdays and several times a week in the summer. My neighbors told me on various occasions that they would hear us singing, which surprised me because I did not think that we were that loud. I felt that our home was covered with prayer and praise. The children and I faithfully attended church and Bible study every week. We attended just about all the special conferences and meetings held at the church. We studied the Bible at home.

Two Daughters Leave

Within a few months of my discovery of the molestation of our daughters, my oldest daughter who I had become her legal guardian from foster care wanted to leave our home. She did not come right out and tell me that she wanted to leave, but her behavior changed. She misbehaved at school. She developed friendships with young men and women who did not go to school and were involved in criminal activity.

Late one afternoon, I received a telephone call from my social worker. He told me that she had accused me of physically abusing her. He informed me that he was going to remove her and her younger sister from my home. I told the social worker that I did not physically abuse her, but I was not opposed to him removing them from my home. As I talked with him, I thought, here is a good opportunity for these two daughters to leave my home.

I informed her younger sister that they were going to be leaving our home and she cried uncontrollably. She did not want to leave me. That day the social worker came and picked up the younger sister and her belongings, along with her sister's clothing that I had packed for her. The oldest girl was not at my home when I received the phone call from the social workers. They were placed in a foster home in a neighboring city. Subsequently, I talked to the youngest sister often, but I had very little contact with the older sister for four years.

Notes

CHAPTER 4

CAN YOU HANDLE THE TRUTH?

Help, Lord!

After a few days of considering my options after Hubert moved out, I informed him that I was going to call the church to seek psychological counseling for the family. I contacted the church and requested to speak to one of the newer pastors on staff. She had recently given up her church by the command of God and came to join our church's staff. She had over 1,000 members, but she was obeying the command of God. She led Morning Prayer, and she led the prayer and praise worship service on Wednesday evenings. Both services helped me get through the most difficult period of my life. They were an answer to the silent cries of my heart.

Before she joined our church, I felt that there was no one on the staff who could help me. The church had thousands of members. I was a faithful member, but I had no personal contact with the pastor or any other pastor on staff. I attended church and Bible study, and I volunteered without ever speaking personally with the pastor. He did not greet people after service during those years. When service was over, he left. This same kind of hands-off approach to those outside of the inner circle was exhibited by the guest speakers at special conferences as well.

A few weeks after I discovered what Hubert was doing, the church had a special guest speaker, and I attended the service. As the speaker was teaching, I started to cry uncontrollably. The more I tried to stop, the harder I cried. I kept wiping my eyes with tissue until I ran out of tissue, then I started wiping my eyes with my sleeves. The people around me gave me tissue, but they did nothing else. They did not try to talk to me or comfort me in any way. The preacher looked directly at me throughout service and said nothing. I felt so embarrassed. I could not stop crying.

When the service was over, I turned and looked back at the guest speaker as I was walking out. There were male ushers and female hospitality ministers who ministered to the guest speaker. They gave him water to drink and a towel to wipe the sweat from his head. The ushers carried his Bible and other belongings for him and escorted him out of the sanctuary. However, no one ministered to me as I cried throughout the entire service. While leaving the sanctuary I asked God, *"Why did you do that to me?"*

I sat in my car for a few minutes before I left, and I thought about how I cried and no ministry staff or volunteer offered to help me in any way. A few women who sat near me offered me tissue to wipe my eyes and nose, but that was all. I was so embarrassed and so defeated that I decided that I was not going go back to that church. But that was not God's plan for me.

The next Sunday my children and I did not go to church; instead, we decided to sleep late. The following Wednesday, God spoke to me all day to attend the prayer and praise service that evening. I decided to obey the voice within me. I dropped the children off at children's church, and I went into service. The atmosphere was filled with praise and worship. I sat in the back of the auditorium to observe the service. Within a few minutes, the new pastor on staff began to speak a word from the Lord about a woman that God was healing a condition with her hair. She touched the top of her head and said, *"Your hair is falling out."* My hair was falling out because the hairstylist had left a curling solution on my hair too long. God had my attention. He revealed to me that he had brought this pastor to our church to minister to me and my family.

From that moment, I decided to attend all of her services. The next morning my children and I attended Morning Prayer at 5 a. m. We entered the room through the rear of the building. As we were walking to the front to be seated, the pastor said, *"There goes a blessed woman."* I looked behind me to see who she was referring to, but there was no one behind us. I thought to myself, how am I blessed? We sat down and listened to her teachings. We attended Morning Prayer all week, Monday through Friday, for months.

I called the church to schedule counseling for my family. I wanted to connect with the pastor whose services I was attending daily, but she was not in that day. I really wanted to connect with someone that day. It had been over four weeks since my husband moved out of the house, and I wanted to move forward with the healing process for my family. I agreed to talk with another minister on staff. The person I spoke with was a medical doctor. I told him what happened. I also informed him that I wanted to get help for my husband and children, but I did not want to go through the system because I did not want my family torn apart. He understood, and he said that he would call me back if he could find someone to help me.

A few hours later, he called me back with the name of a prominent psychiatrist who was willing to work with us. I called him and set up an appointment for my husband and me to meet with him. I informed him that Hubert had moved out of the house. We met the following week and the psychiatrist scheduled counseling sessions for each member of our family and some joint sessions for my husband and I to attend together.

The sessions were emotionally draining. I listened to the doctor describe the profile of a pedophile. He gave me information to read and then asked me questions about what I had read. Then we discussed how I felt about it. My emotions were high. I was extremely hurt, disappointed and confused that my husband would turn from me to a child. My self-esteem was at the lowest point that it had ever been in my life. The magnitude of the problem and the circumstances surrounding it became overwhelming. Not only could I not bear children, but my husband was attracted to the children that I had brought into our home. I thought they were there to help satisfy our need to be parents and their need for parents, but he abused them for his own selfish sexual gratification.

I questioned my husband about what motivated him to commit such acts, but he was unable to give me an answer. He said he did not know why. The psychiatrist could not give me a conclusive answer. I asked God why, but I did not hear an answer. I assumed the answer lay in the fact that we could not have children of our own, that somehow the desire for my husband to obtain the unobtainable for himself had turned into a psychosexual disorder. In the back of my mind, I felt that I had somehow caused this sickness to manifest by bringing children into our home. Therefore, I was determined to help him overcome this disorder by the power of God using medical and spiritual means. However, I would only do it if he were willing to do whatever was necessary to achieve his healing and deliverance.

My children and I met with the doctor for six months. My husband continued meeting with the doctor for an additional six months until the doctor released him. My husband and I remained separated, but he continued to support us financially. During and after his release from treatment he visited us two to three days a week. He did not sleep in our home, nor was he alone with the children at any time. A few months before he was released by his psychiatrist, I allowed him to transition back into our home. The transition started with weekend visits for two months, and then he moved back into our home the third month. However, my lack of complete trust in him started to become unbearable. My distrust motivated me to make a decision that ultimately placed our family in chaos.

My Third Prophetic Encounter

Three years passed and our family was still holding together, but I was under tremendous stress. At the beginning of year three, I noticed a change in Hubert's behavior. I did not think that he was molesting our daughters. It was the little things that made me uncomfortable. He started staying up late at nights. He started playing that disturbing music again. Hubert liked writing and playing his own songs, and he brought musical instruments, and he learned computer music or midi music. He composed music that made me angry and nervous when I listened to it. This music was the same type of music that he played when he was alone late at night. I asked him to go back to counseling because I noticed the changes in his behavior and he played that music, but he refused. He said he was fine and that he did not need more counseling, but I was not fine.

As the girls got older, I felt that they needed more counseling, but I did not want to go back to Hubert's psychiatrist. I thought they would progress better with a female counselor. I watched Hubert stay up late at nights and play his music until I could not take it any longer. I asked him one final time to go back into counseling. I also told him that I wanted to get the girls more counseling as well. Again, he refused.

My Secret Revealed

In 1996, I decided to get further counseling for my daughters. I had been living the "secret" for five years, and I was stressed out. I wanted spiritual guidance and experienced help in handling my family situation. I wanted to get my girls counseling without destroying my family. I knew that this time Children's Services would be involved, but I wanted to have our situation packaged and presented perfectly so that I would not lose my children. Five years had passed since the incident of sexual contact with our daughters, and I was concerned about Hubert, but I was more concerned about our daughters. Furthermore, I thought that since he received counseling and no other sexual contact had occurred, he would be all right. I thought that the person helping us would counsel us on what we should do, but that did not happen.

I left the mega church and began attending a much smaller church of a few hundred. After two or three months of attending the church, I talked with the pastor about my family situation and asked him to help me. I told him my concerns. He called in his wife, who was also a pastor. He said that she had more experience in my area of concern. He was a new senior pastor. That was my first red flag, which I ignored in my desperation for help and change.

I immediately began having that feeling of worry and dread. His wife came into the meeting. I told her my story, and she said that she had someone who could help me. That was my second red flag. The feelings of worry and dread grew worse. She called the counselor, who was a friend, and placed her on speakerphone. She paraphrased my story and the counselor agreed to help me. She gave me the counselor's telephone number and told me that I was in good hands.

I left the church office more terrified than I had been since I first discovered that Hubert was molesting our daughters. I had confided in strangers. They were people who did not know me or my family, and I revealed to them a family secret that they were obligated to report by law. I had an intense, overwhelming feeling that I had gone to the wrong people for help. I went to my car and sat there holding my chest and clinching the car seat. I had done it again. I made a huge mistake. I did not call the counselor, but I knew that I could not ignore her for long.

Hubert's behavior did not change. He continued to stay up late at night and play his music. I grew more and more fearful. I was afraid to move forward because I kept having that feeling of dread. I could not talk with the pastor or his wife because I felt that they did not want to have anything to do with us.

Fear had paralyzed me. I tried to think rationally about this new situation that I had created. Every time I thought about the pastor, his wife and the counselor I would get this awful feeling of dread. I continued to try to persuade Hubert to go back to counseling. He began to look at me in anger because he believed he was not doing anything wrong. I needed to talk with someone, but it was difficult to discern who to trust. I could not talk with my family. I did not trust that they would keep the information confidential.

The pressure began to affect my behavior. My hands began to shake constantly because of my nervousness. I would hold my hands together and turn them to try and keep them from shaking. The pastor at church noticed the shaking and would look at me strangely. Others also noticed my behavior change, but neither the pastor nor anyone else said anything to me.

God brought in a visiting women's ministry to the church. The woman that I met through this ministry would invite me to go to special conferences and seminars with her, where I received information and ministry that helped me. I did not share my secret with them. They helped me by simply showing me that they cared. After one of the conferences, I made the decision to move forward and begin to seek healing.

Deception

I contacted the counselor and she scheduled an appointment for me to meet with her to begin the process of moving forward. We met and discussed counseling for my daughters. Then the scenario that I dreaded began to unfold. I spoke with the counselor several times and she informed me that she had to report the incident to the Department of Children's Services.

She reviewed the process with me. The plan was for her to be identified as our family counselor. I reminded her that the abuse happened five years prior and that my entire family received counseling. At that time, I was just seeking additional counseling for my daughters. I also reminded her that my husband was currently living in the home with us, but that he had received counseling for over a year with a licensed psychiatrist. In my intensely stress filled mental state, I did not see the need for Hubert to leave before I reported him. The counselor did not advise me that he should leave before she reported him. She never indicated that anything negative would happen to my husband, my children or me as a result of her reporting the abuse with him still in the home.

I went home and told Hubert what I had done. He was surprised. All he could do was look down. Within two hours, a social worker from the Department of Children's Services was at our front door. I invited her in and began to tell her my story. She seemed genuinely empathetic. She called her supervisors to ask what to do, since our case was so unusual. She talked with someone for a few minutes, then hung up the telephone and informed me that they would call her back in a few minutes.

My counselor did not tell me that Hubert should not be living in the home. If she had told me, I would have made sure his belongings were packed and out of the house. When the social worker came to our home and saw my husband there, the community in which we lived, and our house she was surprised. She did not know what to do. We were not the "typical" case or family they were used to dealing with in this type of situation. She called her supervisors for advice, but they were also puzzled. The social worker sat in my house for five hours while her supervisors tried to figure out what to do. Finally, her supervisors, not knowing what else to do, called the police. They supposedly had not dealt with our type of situation before.

As I look back, I believe that the supervisors were waiting for me to realize that Hubert needed to leave, but I was too emotionally upset to think clearly. No one told me he should leave. They asked me for the name of the psychiatrist who helped us, and we refused to disclose the name of his psychiatrist. We did not want to get him in trouble. More time passed, but the social worker still did not tell me that Hubert should not be living in our home. I was blind to what was so obvious. If I had known, Hubert would have left with his suitcases in her presence. She said that she was at our home for such a long period of time because she had people trying to find a home and neighborhood that was compatible to ours. The social worker was on and off of the phone for hours. Then she received a phone call from the supervisor who told her to remove the children.

I was devastated. The police arrived after she told me that my children were going to be removed. The social worker and the police stayed at our home for another hour because they had not located a home for our children. Why were they taking our children? My thinking was so clouded that I could not comprehend that the children were leaving because Hubert was living in the house. The police did not say that he needed to leave. The counselor did not tell me that he needed to leave before she made her report. I believe the process to remove my children took so long because God was trying to communicate with me, but I could not hear him. I was overwhelmed with stress, grief, frustration, fear and a deep feeling of betrayal.

All three of my children were taken that night, my two daughters and my son. As long as I looked within and depended on the God-in-me for answers, everything seemed to work out for me. When I looked outside of me for answers from other people, I lost my children. From that moment on, I decided that I would not trust anyone that I did not know, especially pastors, leaders and counselors in the church.

The police did not arrest my husband that night. He was arrested weeks later. We were not ready. I did not know who to trust. I prayed and asked God to release me from the church, but God refused. My husband and I were paralyzed. We did not try to get a lawyer. We did not call our family for help. We were in shock.

The pastors did not ask me anything else about the issue until well after my children were taken. I purposely did not say anything to them because I wanted to see if they would even notice that I was in church without my children. I always had my children with me at every service, two and three times a week. But for over a month my children had not been with me, and they did not ask me one question about it or inquire further into my dilemma.

Lambs for the Slaughter

Hubert and I ultimately went to court about our children. We found ourselves making mistake after mistake after mistake. One day the social worker called, and I was not at home. Hubert answered the phone. She asked him if he was going to stay in the home. He said, yes. Two days later, we appeared in court. We did not have legal representation, and we were completely unprepared for what the social worker planned against us.

The Department of Children's Services alleged that I had put our children in danger. They presented the charges against us as if the sexual abuse were ongoing. The judge removed our children for 30 days. During that time, the police prepared to arrest Hubert. Two weeks later, the Sheriff's office called and told Hubert to turn himself in. He was arrested for felony child abuse and held on one million dollars bail.

I was stunned. I sat at my dining room table alone, in my empty house for days. Then one day the doorbell rang. It was Hubert's brother just dropping by for a visit. I told him the short version of the story - Hubert molested our daughters and I turned him in. He is in jail now and he needs a lawyer. His brother said okay, and he turned and left.

About two hours later, Hubert called and asked me to call his job and inform them that he had been arrested for an outstanding warrant and that he was going be in jail for at least a week. I asked him how he was doing. He said that he was all right. I told him that I was coming to visit him, but he did not want me to come there. He said, *"I don't want you exposed to this."* I told him that his brother had come by the house and that I told him that he had been arrested and the reason.

The next day, Hubert called and told me that his other brother had retained a lawyer for him and they were on the case. The attorney was a childhood friend of the family. He was the lead attorney in a very successful and respected law firm. Hubert was held in the local jail for two weeks and then was moved to another facility for his arraignment. At the arraignment, I was interviewed by a court clerk who asked me what I wanted to be done to my husband. I said that I did not want him arrested and put in jail. If I wanted that, I would have done it five years prior when I first discovered what he had done. I told the clerk that I was responsible for his arrest because I wanted to get my daughters more counseling.

I informed the clerk that he had not touched our daughters in five years. I also informed him that our entire family had received counseling from a prominent psychiatrist and that Hubert remained in treatment for over a year. He asked me for the psychiatrist's name, but I did not reveal it because we had promised the psychiatrist that we would not disclose his name. He wanted to know why I did not go back to the psychiatrist. The girls were older and I thought they would feel more comfortable with a female counselor. I said, *"I went to Social Services for help, not to be prosecuted as a criminal and certainly not for the Department of Children's Services and the police to destroy the family that I was desperately trying to keep together."*

The clerk left the room where I was sitting. A few minutes later, my husband's attorney came in to talk to me. This was our first time meeting. He introduced himself and gave me his business card. Then he explained the process to me. He told me that Hubert had made a mistake in confessing that he had molested our girls, but that he would handle it. He said that he had filed a writ to have Hubert's bail reduced to the time served. Even though he had confessed he would file something later to have the confession reduced or removed.

We entered the courtroom. Hubert's attorney was highly respected. He walked over and shook hands first with the judge and then with the prosecutors, who all knew his name. I was very impressed by his overall confidence and professionalism. He did exactly what he said. A few days later, Hubert was released from jail.

Judgment in the Church

After the initial court session, I continued to attend church. I did not tell anyone about what happened in court. I would go to church and leave, or I stayed at home and thought about how stupid I was to ask people who I did not know for help in a criminal matter even though they were my pastors. I should have sought the advice of an attorney. If only I had thought about an attorney from the start, we would not have lost everything. We lost our children, our home and our business. We were financially depleted and homeless. Actually, the children and I were homeless. Hubert was living with his mother.

Prior to this incident, I had a very high opinion of pastors. I thought they had a very close connection with God, at least a greater connection than I had. I thought that between God, the pastor, and me we could solve anything. But I was wrong. God and I can solve anything when I listen and obey the voice of the Spirit of God within me. When I looked outside of myself and sought the advice of others to guide me, my family was separated. I learned the hard way that everyone has their own personal opinions, beliefs, prejudices and dislikes that can affect the way they help me if they choose to help at all.

My husband's counselor warned him that there would be people who would never accept him or believe that he was a changed man and that he would have to accept it and stay away from them. The first lady of the church that I joined was one of those people. She drove him out of the church by preaching our business from the pulpit on three separate Sundays. She would look around the church and locate us in the congregation, then she would start talking about child abusers and sex offenders and our confidential information. She would see us looking at her, but she would say, *"I am not talking about anyone specific."* However, she would look directly at my husband when she started talking and during most of her commentary.

My husband endured this verbal assault and violation of our confidentiality on three occasions. The third time she started talking about him from the pulpit was the last time. He left the church that Sunday and did not return. That was over 20 years ago, and he has not been to church since that day.

After my husband left, her husband, the senior pastor, began talking about me from the pulpit in church and at special meetings. He talked about me so often that I scheduled a meeting with him, and I asked him to stop talking about my personal life from the pulpit. He denied talking about me, but I was prepared. I reminded him of the dates that he talked about me, and I told him some of the things that he said. I asked him to listen to the recordings of those services, and he would hear it for himself. I did not leave the church because I believed that the Lord wanted me to stay there. My disobedience had caused all the problems and chaos in our lives, and I was determined not to be disobedient anymore. Therefore, I took the Pastor's verbal abuse for two Sunday's; then, I confronted him about what he was doing.

From that point forward the pastor did not talk about me openly in church, but his wife continued. I had to ask the pastor to ask her to stop talking about me from the pulpit. She would talk about me like she talked about my husband. She would see me in the congregation, and she would describe me by saying, *"There is a woman here whose children are not with her or not living with her;"* or she would talk about my physical demeanor. I may have been crying or sad because of what I had gone through that week or because the presence of God was upon me. I would look up at her and pray, *"God, do you see her? God, do you hear her?"* She would see me looking at her and she would say the same thing that she said when my husband was with me. *"I am not talking about any specific person. I am talking about a situation outside of this church."*

The only thing that she did not reveal was my name, which did not matter because she revealed who I was by her description and constant looking at me as she talked. After I talked with the pastor about his wife's comments, she continued to make comments about me from the pulpit but not as obvious. She would still look for me in the congregation, make one or two brief comments about me, then she would move on with her church related announcements.

I found out months later that she had instructed most of the leaders in the church not to have anything to do with me. Before my husband left, she told her daughter and son-in-law not to have anything to do with either my husband or me. Her son-in-law and daughter told us this information themselves when they talked to us one Sunday after church.

For a long time, I wondered why I had the feeling that I was not liked or wanted in the church by many leaders. I thought that something was wrong with me. As a volunteer working in the baptism area, I noticed that some leaders stared at me before the prayer by the elders and ministry workers. The leaders' actions were passive/aggressive towards me. They tolerated me, but they really did not want to work with me. One of the leaders opened the Sunday service with prayer and led praise and worship. In fact, several leaders who felt this way towards me were in the choir and members of the music ministry.

A few weeks later, God revealed through a visiting prophet that these same men and women in the choir and those leading praise and worship including several musicians and other ministry leaders were involved in active adultery with each other or another member of the church or with someone outside of the church. The pastors announced in a Sunday service that adultery and fornication was occurring in the leadership of the ministry and the prophet revealed the individuals who were involved. They announced their names and their punishment. Several church leaders lost their ministry positions permanently because they had committed sexual improprieties in the church prior to their current adulterous relationship. Others were required to sit down for a few months. The pastor's wife and associate pastor's son-in-law was among the group. The current senior pastor was her second husband. She was a widow before they married. Her former husband and senior pastor had sexual affairs with men in the church. I learned months later that the church was known for the senior pastor's sexual exploits and the sexual misconduct of other church members. Before I knew this, I was confused by the associate pastor's apparent hatred of me and my husband that she passed on to her church leaders and her immediate family members.

Something's Wrong

At that time, I did not understand why ministry leaders were acting odd. I was bothered that so many people in the church acted strange towards me. They did not at first. They were kind and caring. I thought that something was wrong with me because I was going through a very difficult emotional battle. I thought that maybe I was acting weird but I did not know it. I talked with my counselor about my feelings and about how I was being treated at church by the pastors and other church leaders. She counseled me in her own soft and gentle style. She reminded me that I did not have to accept mistreatment by anyone or any group of people.

Nevertheless, God commissioned me to continue to attend the church and volunteer in ministry. Once God revealed to me the hypercritical behavior and judgments of the pastors and other church leaders, I understood their passive/aggressive attitude. The leaders who were involved in their own sexual sins chose to hide them and continue in them. My presence probably made them feel uncomfortable because they knew that their transgressions were going to be revealed sooner rather than later. Sooner is exactly what happened when God sent the prophet to the church.

God brought me to a church that was full of people, including leaders who were committing sexual sin of various types. God revealed to me that I was not the only church leader with sexual secrets in my life. I had revealed my own secret, and I was dealing with the consequences, one of which involved my children remaining in foster care for another six months.

The Disclosure Agreement

My children were in foster care for six months. During that time, I continued to go to church without them. After three weeks had passed and not one word had been said to me concerning my children, I met with the pastor. I wanted to update him on my case. I really wanted to see his reaction when I told him that I had lost my children and why. While I was waiting to go in for my appointment, I was given a disclosure agreement to sign. I was told that before I could meet with the pastor I needed to read and sign it. The pastor's assistant informed me that the pastor required everyone to sign a disclosure agreement before meeting with him. I held the form in my hand and looked at it closely without reading it. I prayed and said, *"Lord, this form is for me because of what was done to me and my family. He is trying to protect the church from future lawsuits, which is good. But my signing this form today will not protect him, his wife and this church if I were to sue them for violating my confidentiality, and for what the counselor that they recommended to me did to my family. This form is an admission to me that my family was mistreated."*

I asked the Lord if I could leave the church for good, but God told me to stay. I was troubled by God's response. I did not understand why He would want me to stay there. I read and signed the disclosure agreement, which included sexual abuse reporting requirements among other crimes that had to be reported to the police if the signee disclosed that information. In the meeting, I told the pastor that my children would not be with me for six months or more. After that meeting, I decided that I would not meet with him about my children anymore, but I did meet with him often to discuss my business.

The Effects of Rejection

God wanted the pastor to help me launch my business. However, he was not interested in giving me the type of business coaching that I needed because of my family problems. I had a great idea to develop and create websites for churches and set-up and manage computer-based learning centers in local churches. Hubert and I had invested a great deal of money in developing the idea. We needed a business mentor to help us set up the business systems that we needed to launch and maintain our business.

I attended various community meetings, preaching that the African American community needed to become computer literate and we needed to be in the forefront of this new computer technology—the Internet. My preaching caught the attention of a prominent owner of two popular Christian bookstores in the community. He introduced me to the leaders of an organization of churches who needed my services. I began working for them as a community organizer part-time for very little pay. God gave me this connection, and I needed a mentor to help me.

Before I destroyed our family, Hubert and I met with the pastor of the church. We showed him pictures that Hubert created of the network that we wanted to develop and market. We talked with him about our ideas and what our software developers were doing for us. He thought it was a good idea. Then I began to think about our family secret. Hubert's change in behavior really concerned me. I wanted the secret to be out in a controlled way so that I could get my daughters and Hubert the counseling they needed, and there would be no secret to come out and ruin us. The more I talked about our business, the more I knew that I had to get rid of that secret, which caused me even more stress. Ultimately, the secret was revealed and it ruined us in more ways than one.

The revelation of our secret devastated our lives in several ways. Our relationship with our pastor and church family was strained. Their personal opinions of us changed, and the assistance that I requested that would help eliminate our secret backfired on our family. We lost our children for 13 months. Hubert went to jail, confessed, and was convicted of felony child sexual abuse. I could no longer trust the pastors to help me with any aspect of my personal life, and they did not trust me either.

5 CHAPTER

UNRAVELING THE STRANGLEHOLD OF GUILT

Paralyzed By Fear

After I lost my family, I was paralyzed by anger, fear, and self-loathing. I did not know what to do or where to go for help. I did not move. I did not follow the court mandates. The systems that we set up for our business were costing us money that we did not have because we were not able to generate new business. Hubert could no longer work in our home, which was our place of business. The leaders of the network of churches that I worked for requested that Hubert no longer work on anything for them.

Hubert was the one who took my ideas and made them a practical reality. I worked for a church-based organization of over 30 churches. From the vision, he created and managed the church organization's website and each member church's individual website. Hubert was innovative and before his time. Unfortunately, our church pastors and the pastors that I worked for rejected us, and they did not want to have anything to do with us. I was very surprised because the church organization was organized around reducing ex-offender crime. In fact, I was part of the working group that met at the County Probation Department's local office to develop the pilot program. The group consisted of leaders from the Probation Department, the District Attorney's Office, the Public Defender's Office, the Superior Court Judge's office, and local congressional district representatives, County Supervisors' representatives, and a representative from a local University as the program evaluators.

When they told me that my husband could not have anything to do with designing and maintaining their organizational website, I considered them to be hypocrites. I understood that they were protecting themselves against a scandal, but I thought the whole purpose behind the work that we were doing was to help ex-offenders, especially those ex-offenders who were doing everything that the court required them to do. In our situation, we did not experience grace, mercy, forgiveness, and tolerance when our secret was revealed from any pastor or church that I attended or worked with in any capacity. They told me to take my gifts, talents, and ideas and leave and not come back.

I felt like we were the "lepers" of the modern-day world. Not even the church wanted us near them. However,

God told me that not all churches felt this way. Nevertheless, my husband and I followed the church organization's request. My husband took his hands off of everything that he had built and established, and I resigned from the church-based nonprofit organization.

For weeks following our departure from the nonprofit organization, I sat at home alone, and I thought about the work that we had accomplished for the organization, the loss of my children, what I had done to my husband, and our inability to pay our mounting bills. I began to give up on my dreams of a home, family, and business. I began to think that it would be best if I left my children in foster care. I thought about how the attorney assigned to my children and Children's Services wanted to permanently strip me of my parental rights.

My Children Were Endanger

For over two months, I allowed negative thoughts to stream through my mind. Then I decided to stop visiting my children. I thought that it would be good for them to get used to not seeing me. I did not call or visit them for six months, and no one called to ask me why until the third month. By the second month of not seeing or hearing from me, my son began to misbehave. He wanted to go home. By the third month, the foster mother was tired of him and she wanted him removed from her home, but she wanted to keep my daughters.

My oldest daughter heard about what the foster mother was trying to do. She refused to stay there without her brother. She wanted all three of them to move together, and she informed the social workers of their desire. Overall, my children were well-behaved children, but my son wanted to go home.

The foster mother and her 19-year-old daughter began mistreating my oldest daughter and son. The foster mother began threatening to have my son sent to another home by himself. Her daughter began calling my son and daughter filthy names. The foster mother disclosed our family business to her family and friends. They talked about me and my husband in the presence of our children. Our children had to endure the humiliation and verbal abuse while I was deciding whether or not I was good enough to continue to be their parent.

The Children's Response

My son and my oldest daughter responded to these mentally intimidating attacks the only way they knew at that time. They began failing in school and rebelling against the foster mother. For example, to punish my son for saying at school that he wanted to go home, the foster mother made him get up before dawn and clean up her backyard in the dark and cold without a sweater or jacket. In response, my son broke her flowerpots. My youngest daughter was able to cope better. She was not a problem for the foster mother. In fact, she was her favorite, and she used her to break my son's toys and tear up his nice clothes. This treatment caused my son and older daughter's behavior to grow even more problematic at school, especially my son. He started disrupting the class.

The social workers began calling me and requesting that I visit my children. They told me that my son was acting out because he missed me and my husband. My son told the social workers that he wanted to see both of us and he wanted to go home. I told the social workers that I would call the foster mother and make an appointment to see my children, but I did not do it. I thought it was in their best interest to remain in foster care and either stay where they were or be placed in another foster home. I felt that I had failed them and that they would be better off living in another home with better parents. I did not visit or call for six months. I was waiting for my children's attorney to do what she said she wanted to do: Take away my parental rights.

My Spiritual Rights

The Spirit of God kept talking to me about my spiritual rights as I sat at home alone, angry and discouraged. At any time, I had the right to get up and take authority over my situation. God kept speaking to me to visit my children and I kept saying that they were better off in foster care. I felt guilty for bringing them into our home and exposing them to my husband's actions. In addition, it appeared that everyone was against me and my husband, especially the pastors of the church where I was a member including many of the church members, the church organization that I had worked for, the social workers, prosecutors, and attorneys working for the Department of Children's Services, and the courts.

I was up against people and governmental entities that had the resources of the church and the State of California behind them. Even Hubert had a good attorney that his family got for him. All I had was a public defender who appeared to be more for the system than for me. God had to remind me that *"greater is he who is within me than he who is in the world,"* and that *"no weapon formed against me can prosper."* God told me that if I endured to the end and did not give up, I would reap a harvest in the right season. In God I had all the resources of heaven behind me. As long as I kept fighting, I would win because God and I were the majority.

I started thinking positive thoughts about the power of God within me. My outlook on life started changing. God began to bring outside ministries to the church that I was attending to help me break the bondage of blame and shame. God even brought my first pastor to the church to preach. After he prayed the opening prayer, he said in a loud voice, *"It is not your fault."* He said it three times at the beginning of his sermon and many times throughout his sermon. I sat there trying not to cry and show weakness among so many people whose eyes were on me.

The Prophetic Word of Life

Shortly after that sermon, God brought a leader in the prophetic ministry to a church where I was attending a women's conference. The prophetic pastor gave me a prophetic word. He told me that the war was over and that my faith had prevailed. He told me to go home and jump three times in every room of my house and what I was facing would be over permanently. I drove home and opened the door jumping. I jumped in every room of my house three times as instructed.

The next day I took Hubert some of his belongings to his mother's house. When he was released from jail he moved in with his mother and two brothers. I gave him his belongings and I told him that things had changed and that I was not going to go through that again. I told him that I stayed with him because I believed that God could heal anything and because of my marriage vow to stay with him in sickness and in health. I reminded him that he agreed to do everything that he needed to do to get healed and delivered. He also agreed to have God in his life and to go to church. I reminded him that he stopped going to church and refused to go back into counseling when I practically begged him to go. I said goodbye and I drove home.

My Decision to Stay Married

The next Sunday, I saw Hubert in church. He was sitting a couple of rows behind me. The pastor asked for people who needed prayer for their marriage to come to the altar. I went to the altar and asked God if I should finally divorce my husband. Then I looked behind me. Hubert had stepped into the aisle and was on his way to the altar on his knees. He was praying and crying and asking God to forgive him. He asked me not to leave him. I looked into his eyes. He reached out his hands towards me. I took them and he stood next to me. The pastor began to pray, then we went back to the pew where I was sitting, and we sat together.

I Finally Called

It was late fall. Thanksgiving and Christmas were coming and I missed my children. God continued to tell me to call my children and to see them. God impressed upon me the urgency to find out what was going on with my son. Finally, I listened. I called my children's social worker and asked her for the foster mother's telephone number. She was willing to give it to me after I answered a series of questions. I did not want to answer any of her questions. I just wanted the telephone number. She repeated that I had to answer her questions first. I remained quiet as I became angrier by the second. She asked me was I still on the phone. I took a deep breath and said that I was still there.

She asked me if I had started the parenting classes ordered by the judge. I said, no. Before she could ask me anything else I told her that I had not completed anything that the court ordered me to do. I was not convicted of anything. Why should I act like I was convicted of a crime? The social worker said, *"The judge has authority over your children, and you will not get them back until you do what she has ordered you to do."* The judge was holding my children hostage until I did what she said. She gave me the foster mother's telephone number. I was still angry after the call, but I knew that I had to let go of my anger, guilt, and pity and do whatever was necessary to get my children back.

My Personal Counselor

God had let me know that things were not good with my children, especially my son. I had to get up and take action. I called my husband's psychiatrist. Hubert went back to the doctor who helped us in the beginning. He counseled Hubert as a part of his court ordered recovery program. I asked him for a referral to a female psychologist for me. I was under less stress and able to think better. He gave me the telephone number to the best psychologist ever as far as I am concerned. I met with her around Thanksgiving. She had her own practice. She was a soft spoken, gentle woman, who was short is stature but a giant in wisdom and compassion.

When I arrived at her office, she invited me in, introduced herself, and directed me to a small room. There were two cushioned chairs on each side of the room directly across from each other, a whiteboard, markers, and an eraser hanging on the wall positioned in the middle of the cushioned chairs, a small bookcase, and a desk for children with stuffed animals. There were several boxes of tissue located around the room and within reach of both of us. As I sat down, I tried to get as comfortable as I could. She sat down across from me with her clipboard and notepaper, and she started telling me about herself.

She was a former teacher and elementary school principal who decided to become a psychologist after working many years with children and their families. She was a licensed child and family therapist and a Doctor of

Education. When she finished telling me about herself, I felt very comfortable and safe. She asked me to tell her why I was there. I do not remember the first question she asked, but I do remember talking and crying, and crying, and crying. When I had finished telling her my story, she stood up and went to the whiteboard. She picked up a marker and began to reveal why I was behaving the way that I was behaving.

As she talked, she listed each one of my psychological responses to the events that had happened to me. It all began to make sense. I began to feel normal. For the first time, I felt that I had someone in my corner; someone who actually wanted to see me win and who sincerely wanted to see me reunited with my children. I began meeting with my psychologist three times a week. I was ordered to complete parenting classes and individual counseling, and she was qualified and licensed to do both.

I told my psychologist about my conversation with my children's social worker. She wrote a letter to Children's Services introducing herself and the services she was providing for me. She also told me that she trained social workers. From that point on, the social workers did not ask me again about my individual counseling or parenting classes. They called my psychologist directly. She also prepared all the court reports for me for the three years that my children and I were under the supervision of Children's Services and Children's Court.

6 CHAPTER

SILENT CRIES OF THE HEART

The Pain of Rejection

I decided to join another church several years later because I missed church and I desired to serve in ministry. I was very hesitant to join. I knew my background, and I knew how people reacted when they heard about my family secret. Nonetheless, I decided to join and get involved in the ministry. I felt led by the Spirit to teach young adults, so I volunteered for the youth ministry. Part of the application asked that you disclose any convictions. I knew they conducted background checks. I was married to a sex offender, so I thought Hubert's offense would somehow appear on my record. I decided to disclose my husband's past so that if it showed up, they would see that I was not trying to conceal information. Before I disclosed, I asked the director if the document was confidential. She said yes. After I disclosed my husband's record, we talked about it briefly. I let her know that I would be the only person from my family to attend the church. I thought that my information was safe.

The Sunday school director decided to disclose the information I shared on the document with several people in the church, one of whom was an associate pastor who was a former social worker supervisor. As a result, they delayed my training. They sent me to various trainings as a process of rejecting me as a Sunday school teacher. I was formerly a church elder and Sunday school teacher. I had credentials to teach adult school, and I had been a teacher for over 16 years. They required me to go through training, which I understood. However, they required me to go through several trainings with various teachers for eight months. I did not teach one Sunday school class or even co-teach.

The last training class that I attended, the ex-social worker supervisor and another gentleman were teaching a class for middle school teenagers. They allowed me to observe and to participate sparingly. At the end of the class, the ex-social worker said, *"By the way, I want to talk to you guys about pedophiles."* I was shocked. In fact, throughout the eight months of training, no instructor taught about sexual abuse. The Sunday school lesson had nothing to do with sexual abuse. She began talking about what the class should do if a man approached them at church in a manner that made them feel uncomfortable and threatened. I sat there in front of the class feeling that this "By the way" presentation was meant more for me than for the class. I felt that my confidentiality had been completely violated. I was in another church ministry where a pastor violated my confidentiality. I was very angry and disappointed. The professionals in the world do not carelessly violate sexual misconduct information. They know that such a violation could mean loss of job and life and other negative consequences for the one whose privacy is violated.

When the associate pastor and retired social worker supervisor finished speaking, I gathered my belongings and decided to leave the church. I did not want to go through this scenario again. I wanted to say something to associate pastor, but I decided not to get into any debates or arguments in front of the children and their parents. However, I did look for the Sunday school director. She was near in the next room over, and I approached her. Before I could speak to her, a group of four other Sunday school teachers surrounded me including the former social worker supervisor. They began talking about pedophiles and not having them in their church. I looked each one in their eyes. I turned and left without saying one word. As I was leaving, I began to speak to God. I said, *"God, you told me that it was going to be different. I know that you know how to handle people like this. You have done it before. I do not have anything else to say. I know you can take care of it."* I had not molested a child, yet they treated me as if I were an unrepentant child molester in their midst. My husband had not attended any church service, yet they spoke like he was there that Sunday morning. I left the whole situation including the violation of my confidentiality in the hands of God.

I was also working with the church's head of Community Development in creating a program that provided high school equivalency classes and job readiness development for ex-offenders. The pastor asked me to move forward with the program and to give a presentation. The Probation Department wanted to launch a pilot program in which volunteers would be available in court to counsel juvenile offenders or ex-offenders and their parents to avoid misunderstandings after court proceedings. I informed the pastor of the opportunity that the Probation Department presented. This was an opportunity to evangelize because we would have a chance to provide community service to the children and their parents.

The executive director asked me to give a presentation to the pastor and members of the program team about the program that we had designed together. I made the presentation to the pastor and the team members. At the end of the presentation and to my surprise, the pastor stood up and said, *"I don't want any ex-offenders in my church. Just forget that part. But I will do the high school equivalency classes with you. In fact, I will give some seed money toward that program."*

I was shocked and disappointed at the pastor's very negative and hostile reaction towards me. He was standing looking down at me with the meanest look of anger. He was the one three weeks before who had asked me to move forward with the program, but he suddenly changed his mind. Not only did he change his mind, but he also rejected the ex-offender portion in such a strong and negative way that he directed at me. I concluded that he believed someone's lie about me, and he did not ask me if the lie was true. I believe that the liar had convinced him that I was trying to bring sexual offenders into their church, including my husband. If he had asked me, I would have told him that my husband vowed not to attend church again. He has kept that vow for over twenty years.

After thinking about the pastor's offer for a couple of weeks and seeking God about what to do, God told me not to do anything with that church or any other church. God said, *"Anything that I call you to do I want you to do on your own. Don't go to a church with it anymore."* I resigned from the church and gave notice to the pastor that I would no longer be able to work with the program. For nearly a year, the retired social worker supervisor and other church staff had worked diligently to remove me from their church. They accomplished their goal, but God was in it for me. I knew that God had favored me, and he gave me the ability to keep moving forward.

I never told anyone about our family struggles until my children were taken from us, and even then, I was reluctant. I did not tell family, church family or friends. I did not trust people with the details of our story. When I finally shared part of the story with my family, many of them turned their backs on us. My youngest brother spread the news to relatives far and wide. No one called. No one checked on us. No one cared. I just wanted to see my immediate family saved. I wanted my family restored. I wanted my family to stay together. As a result, I had to sacrifice my extended family, friends and even my social life.

However, Hubert's family was more supportive. His brothers still came over to our house to visit. Our relationship with them did not change. His mother was disappointed when she first heard what Hubert had done, but she forgave him. I was able to go to her for advice and comfort when I could not talk to my own mother. Even though my mother still had nuggets of wisdom that she could share with me, I chose not to burden her with the difficult dilemma that I faced. Unfortunately, years later my husband's mother and his oldest brother died within 30 days of each other. The loss was devastating for both Hubert and me. They were our support group. They were what we called our "no judgment zone." We lost two people who were very important to us in our lives as a whole and to our healing process.

Some Sins Are Just Too Hard

I have learned that sexual abuse, pedophilia, and child molestation is a very volatile subject and most people are not able to handle the topic. Although many people say they can handle it, especially church leaders and Christians in general, judgment, negative opinions, and hatred always seem to take over. I have been hurt by family and friends. I have been disappointed, rejected and betrayed by Christian leaders.

At one point in my life, I wanted to isolate myself and my family. I wanted to be as far away from people as I possibly could so that I could avoid the hurt, disappointment and frustration that I experienced when people did not meet my level of expectation for them. I had resolved within myself that if this is how people are going to treat us, then I would hold everything close to my heart and not share it. I had to protect myself and my family from any further hurt.

My husband and I decided to sit in the background of life. We lived in our own little, isolated world. He had some friends that he could still socialize with, but he chose not to socialize with them. My husband did not step foot in a church or communicate with any pastor or church leader for over 20 years. We were very particular about who came around us.

However, there came a point in my life that I no longer wanted to hide. I chose to remain married to my husband. It was a conscious decision. It was my decision. I chose to walk through the fire with him. I chose to keep my family together. I chose to fight and fight in public. I no longer cared what people thought. I did not care how people felt. I was determined not to back down. If people did not like me because I chose to stay with my husband and save my family, then they had to deal with that on their own. Yes, we made mistakes along our journey to regain hope, but we remained together.

The God of a Second Chance

My foundation is God. I love God. I trusted God in every situation that we faced; however, I had to learn how to trust God at deeper levels to move through the difficult process of recovery from all the mistakes and regrets that I and Hubert had. My struggle came from the servants of God that He brought into our lives. Church leaders treated my husband like he was the worst person in the world. They had no compassion, no forgiveness, and no love for him or me. They did not offer us membership into their support system that would embrace my husband and our family with love and then help us achieve healing, wholeness and completeness in God. God offers salvation to everyone, but some churches and their pastors do not.

Is there a standard operating procedure for pastors? Isn't the church supposed to embrace all of God's children, regardless of what sin they have committed? Are those who commit sexual sins beyond forgiveness by the Heavenly Father and by man especially men and women who have gone through the criminal justice system, completed sexual abuse programs, and are doing everything that the law has required them to do? They are not offending children and some have lived law abiding lives for over twenty years as was my husband's case. Are these men and women not candidates for forgiveness? Can they be allowed in church like all other former sinners to live out their redemption and their salvation? Are there any truly Godlike people who are not afraid and filled with hatred who are willing to disciple and be a friend to the ex-child sexual offender. Many of these men and women are not the monsters that people think they are. They may be their own son and daughter.

Many people who have committed horrendous and displeasing sins have tried to join a congregation of people who say they love the Lord and claim that God can do anything, but their attitude is quite different if they know your business. Some pastors and senior leaders claim that God is everything, but then they choose who they want to be a part of their congregation, and then some pastors use underhanded tactics to drive out individuals that they do not want in the church. Me and my family would have been better off and grateful if the first pastor and his wife would have told us "we do not want you here, now leave." This is exactly what the second pastor and is ex-social worker supervisor did with me. The ex-social worker and other Sunday School teachers surrounded me like a gang of women, who were determined to get me out of their church in anyway necessary even though I had done nothing wrong except in their eyes. I stayed with my husband as I vowed to do in sickness and in health when we were married. I left that church and I did not go back.

The Lord saved me and my family in spite of the many hardships and adverse judgments that we had to endure. One of the things that I had to endure was five years of supervision by the Department of Children and Family Services, which coincided with the five-year probation that my husband was serving. There are no accidents or coincidences. In my family's case, everything that me and my husband endured was intentional. We made it through. We stayed married for 25-years after my husband's probation was over, and the Department of Social Services closed my case. We stayed married until his untimely death. He allowed grief, sorrow, guilt, and regret to consume him after certain family members learned about his past sin nearly twenty-years later, and they told everyone that would listen about it. My husband was so hurt that everyone knew that he had sexually molested our daughters. He could not face people, and he refused to go with me to any family function or event. He stayed at home with the pets. He died ten years after our enemies revealed our family secret. Then I had to deal with my guilt and grief because I had disobeyed the Lord's warning so many times not to adopt our children, especially the girls, but I did not listen and obey. I thought that if only I listened, he would still be alive, and we would have led different lives, and the children as well.

CHAPTER 7

WHEN IT'S ALL SAID AND DONE

True Redemption

"In Him we have redemption (deliverance and salvation)
through His blood, the remission (forgiveness) of our
offenses (shortcomings and trespasses), in accordance with
the riches and the generosity of His gracious favor."
(Ephesians 1:7)

"Redemption," according to Webster's Dictionary, is defined as, *"to make better or more acceptable; to exchange for money, an award; to buy back."*

God told me not to adopt my daughters. At the time, I did not understand why he did not want me to have children in my home. But God was trying to save me, my husband, and our children from the hurt and pain that we suffered because of my decision not to obey God. God knew the sickness that lied dormant in my husband's mind. The adoption of my daughters just activated this sickness that had been asleep in a deep place of his soul.

For years, I blamed myself because I refused to hear and obey God. Even though I had not sexually abused my daughters, I felt that I had created the space for my husband to make the wrong choices. Therefore, I felt that it was my responsibility to get him the help that he needed to recover. I married him "for better or worse," and when it is all said and done, I am partly responsible for keeping our covenant intact.

God redeemed me through His son, Jesus Christ. He forgave all of my sins. Therefore, I can forgive my husband. When I think about redemption, I also think about the water and the blood of Jesus. The water is knowing what to do, but the blood is actually doing what you know, especially under very difficult circumstances. To keep myself going, I cast down all negative thoughts that produced anger, violence, and hatred through the power of God within me. This was a job that I worked hard at every day through prayer and praise.

The Bible says we have to work out our own salvation with fear and trembling (Philippians 2:12). Yes, Jesus saved me, but there were some things that I had to work out on my own through Christ. When I accepted Jesus Christ as my personal savior, I became a new person in Christ Jesus. The old man had passed away and the new man was emerging (2 Corinthians 5:17).

In order for me to walk in that newness of life, I had to do mental work. I dismantled the old thoughts and cast down the old imaginations whenever they surfaced in my mind. It took mental work not to wallow in self-pity and beat myself up because of my mental blindness. I worked hard to resist those thoughts and replace them with positive thoughts through study and meditation of the Bible and other self-help materials.

I wanted to be able to forgive my husband like Christ forgives us, but it was a process. Sometimes I would just lay in bed and quote scripture. I would find a chapter that related to my situation, and I would memorize it. I would quote chapter after chapter to myself. Sometimes I would read aloud; other times I would speak the Word in my head. I had enough scripture inside of me that I could stay awake for hours, if I needed to, and meditate on God's word.

God saved me and God saved my husband because I trusted God, and God worked out our salvation. The workout process involved attending counseling. I sat down and listened to people say things about me that I did not like and with which I did not agree. However, I did not quit. I allowed God to redeem me through this process. I had to apply God's word to daily situations over and over again until I felt and saw the change. This mental work caused me to push past the tears of sorrow and regret and confront the real issue in front of me—allowing God to make all things new.

God says that we are more than conquerors (Romans 8:37). We are well able to overcome any adversity. We are able to regain our hope in the midst of any and every adverse condition. God made me some promises as a little girl that have yet to come to pass because I refused to move. There is some unfinished business God wants to finish concerning me. Part of the redemption process involved my willingness to be open to discuss and solve the difficult issues in my life that plagued me for years.

No Pain, No Gain

Healing is a process. I had to endure a level of pain in order to reach a point of healing and wholeness. I had to be willing to walk through the grimacing stages of painful truth in order to gain the fullness and freedom that I wanted. I am still in the process of healing. In order for me to be completely healed I have to stop hiding. I have to get out there and tell the truth.

For years, I had a testimony that could not be screamed from the rooftops because there were lives that would be affected and changed. My husband would have lost his job. My children would have been affected. But today, I have to share the story so that others can be set free, healed and delivered. My journey to healing has been a challenge, but maybe I can shorten the distance for others.

Winning the Sexual Abuse War

I wanted to defeat the devil, that state of consciousness that my husband allowed to control his life.

My husband gave himself over to the evil desires that were produced by that consciousness; as a result, he molested our daughters to gratify his desires. I wanted to obliterate that state of consciousness that caused him to molest our daughters. I knew that in Christ Jesus that state of consciousness had already been defeated.

I believed what God said about me in the Bible. God said that I am more than a conqueror in Christ Jesus. (Romans 8:37) God said that he always causes me to triumph in Christ Jesus (2 Corinthians 2:14). In fact, God said that I am a world overcomer through my faith in Christ Jesus (1 John 5:4). No weapon formed against me can prosper (Isaiah 54:17).

As far as I was concerned, I had already won. All I had to do was take my eyes off of the situation in the natural and keep my eyes fixed on Jesus the author and finisher of my faith. I did not care about what anyone else thought about me at that time. I was in a battle. I did not have time to care about the opinions of people who could not help me. Moreover, only two opinions mattered, and they were mine and God's. God said that he would give me the desire of my heart if I believed in that desire without doubting. I believed God. I believed in my desire. Therefore, I was determined to see it in the flesh, my victory.

My goals were to protect our children and help my husband if he really wanted to be helped. These goals replaced my intense need for children. I was determined to save our family. I thought about the vows that my husband

and I promised to each other, *"In sickness and in health, till death do us part."* I wondered whether my husband was very, very sick, or was he very, very evil? I concluded that he was a little of both, but more sick than evil.

I thought about him going to jail. In the long run, what benefit would it be for him to spend five or ten years in jail? Would it make our situation better? Would it change what he did and the damage that he had caused? Would prison make him a better person? I thought about the years that we had been together before I decided to bring foster children into our home. I thought about the three children that we adopted. I thought about the good times and the bad times. I concluded that during the years before we had children in our home the good outweighed the bad.

I also thought about the years that we had children living in our home. For most of those years, he was fine. Should I judge his whole life based on his present mistakes, even though he did the unimaginable? Since it was not revenge that I was seeking but deliverance and healing for everyone, I thought about what would be the best option for our family. I concluded that the whole family needed deliverance and counseling, and not just any regular counseling. We needed specific counseling for a specific deliverance to save our souls.

Why Did I Stay?

I stayed in my marriage because I wanted to save my family. I considered the attack on my children a personal attack on me. It was a spiritual attack. The devil had infiltrated my home and attacked me through my weakness, which was my children, and he used my husband to do it. I was angry, hurt, and offended. I considered myself at that time to be a very spiritual person. I prayed and read my bible daily. I went to church and Bible study each week. I supported every special project and campaign. I paid my tithes faithfully. I listened to every teaching on faith that I could access. I read and listened to all of my pastor's materials and all of the materials of his inner circle of mentors.

I also stayed married because I considered the question, "If the roles were reversed, how I would want my husband to treat me?" Would I want him to leave and abandon me even though I committed this horrible act? How would I want to be treated? Then I thought that God does raise the dead. If God can raise the dead, what can he do with a person who is still alive? I asked God, *"God, if you can raise the decomposing dead, can't you do something with the living dead?"* I decided if he really wants to change, if he is willing to do everything that is required of him, if he wants to remain with me, then I will work with him to save our marriage and put this nightmare behind us.

The truth of the matter is, I still loved my husband. I had been with him since I was 16 years-old, and up to that point he had taken very good care of me. He has always given me whatever I desired, and he gave me the freedom to do whatever I wanted to do. Even though some of the decisions that I made hurt us, he still allowed me to make them. I loved my husband, and I wanted to help him. Plus, I made the vow that I would stand with him in sickness and in health.

My husband was sick, and he had committed this terrible act. My question was, how can I help him with God's help? I believed there was nothing too hard for God. I believed that God would do anything for me. So, the question of whether he could be cured or never entered my mind. I always believed that in God anything was possible. I could believe God for anything, and he would do it for me.

Furthermore, it seemed easier to turn my back and say, *"Okay, that's that. I am done."* But I looked at it as an opportunity to demonstrate the power of God in my life. I remember praying, *"If he is willing to do what he needs to do, then bring it, because I can do anything in God."* I said, *"Lord, let's do this thing."* That was my attitude. I did not care what anybody thought at the time. I was taught that when you are in a fight there is no time for crying and whimpering. You have to get up and do what you need to do. That was my mindset, to get up and do what I needed to do.

Back when my children were taken from me, I thought that I could have walked away. I could have left and thrown in the towel. My children had been taken; I was hurt;

my husband was in jail; I was alone. I could have easily walked away. But I decided to stay and win the battle. There were times when I operated in fear. I had not told anyone, and I did not want anyone to find out. I had worked so hard putting my family together, and I just could not face seeing it torn apart. My intention was always to save my family, and I was going to do whatever was necessary to make that happen as long as my husband was going to do what he needed to do.

From our viewpoint in the beginning, he did what he needed to do. He allowed me to report him to the authorities without any resistance. He confessed. He went to jail for a short period of time. He remained on probation. He went through counseling and other programs. He isolated himself from his family and took himself out of the public eye. God was working in our situation.

If we are faithful to God, God will show himself faithful to us. Psalm 144:1 says, *"Blessed be the LORD my strength which teaches my hands to war, and my fingers to fight."* I had been faithful to God for 15 years, and now God was being faithful to me. I had to take a mental stance in the midst of a difficult situation. The victory was already mine, but I had to be able to endure until the end.

Keep Your Eyes on God

We had to sacrifice everything. At the time, I didn't think I was sacrificing everything. At the time, I thought that I was holding on to everything. Instead of telling our family and friends, we retreated to our own space. We did not associate with anyone who had young children. We stopped socializing with family and friends.

As long as I kept my eyes focused on God, I was able to "walk on water" in the deep with God. But as soon as I turned my eyes to man to help me, I sank. You have to stay focused. God is able to transform any situation. He is able to restore the hope, the joy and the happiness that my husband and I once shared. I wanted back the man that I married, the person who smiled a lot, the person who had hope for a bright and successful future, not the person he had become.

Indoctrinated in my faith. I believed that there was nothing that God could not do. I believed that God had a hedge of protection around me, even though I had put a big hole in it with my disobedience; my failure to hear and obey God. I believed that God had forgiven me, and God would heal my husband, our entire family, and restore a complete hedge of protection around us. Forgiveness was the key to restoration for me and my family, and restoration began with me.

CHAPTER 8

LETTING GO

A Heart That Forgives

In spite of the most difficult process of my life, I can say that I forgave my husband, and everything seemed well with us. Then my evil family members learned about the sexual molestation of our daughters that happened 23 years before they knew about it. They hated me, but they could not touch me because of Hubert and his family's old neighborhood connections. Instead, they focused on Hubert, and they told everyone in and out of state what he had done. They attacked a man who had been their friend for nearly 40 years, and who had not tried to hurt them in any way until they tried to hurt me. Then through other family members, he told them not to try it, and they listened because they knew what they would be facing. After they spread Hubert's past mistake around to everyone they could, my evil family members were spared from retribution by Hubert who told those who loved him not to do what they had planned for his and my sake. Hubert demonstrated that he still loved me even though he was angry at me for ruining our lives. He also kept the promise he made to his mother to be the peacemaker in the family. Yes, I ruined our lives in two primary ways.

First by disobeying the Lord who told me not to adopt our daughters and to give them back to the Department of Child Services but I did not do it. Secondly, the process of fixing what had happened caused Hubert and me to give up everything in our lives including our hopes and dreams before we brought little girls into our home. Moreover, what we did not give up, we lost. We lost our home, our privacy, our savings. However, most of all, Hubert lost himself in self-hatred. This kind and generous man who was funny and fun who was filled with joy and laughter allowed himself to become a very sad alcohol abuser. He was not verbal or physically abusive to me or anyone else except himself. I prayed for Hubert's deliverance, but my prayers were not answered by God on purpose.

Whenever Hubert asked me for money to buy alcohol, I gave it to him because it was his money; instead, I should have left him, but I did not. I felt responsible for what had happened to him. I know that he was responsible for his own life and the choices that he made. However, his choice to adopt children was made to please me because he could not give me children, and he blamed himself. Therefore, he tried to make up for his inability by giving me his love and everything else that he could afford that I wanted. Unlike

Hubert, I was very selfish. I did not do what was in his best interest when he began drinking before he damaged his body beyond doctor's abilities to help him. If I would have left him then, I believe that our lives would have been much different. He may have lived a much fuller and happier life. I wanted victory my way with him living with me, but he may have needed to get away from me and all of the negative memories that he had to endure living with me. He would not pack his suitcases and leave me on his own, but I could have left. He wanted and needed to be free of me and all of the child molestation baggage that came with staying with me. His psychiatrist advised him to leave me and not look back or else he would always be facing the memories of the molestation and looking upon the daughters that he molested, but he would not leave me and I would not let him go. In the end, he did go.

After seven years of over-drinking, Hubert died from alcohol abuse. He destroyed his heart and other internal organs. Now, I ask myself the question, "Why did Hubert and I go through all that we went through if he was going to give up and die?" My answer is that I did not let him go when I should have. I should have trusted God to take care of him, but I did not. For that reason, I no longer have him with me. Hubert's death is one of my biggest regrets, but like the other regrets that I have, I must leave them in the past if I want to have a future in the Lord here on earth. Forgiving myself and letting go of my past has been the hardest challenge of my life. In those time, I remind myself that I am not going to give into defeat. I was not born to come to earth and be defeated by the enemy so badly. Hubert is dead. However, I am still alive, and I want to complete the assignment that the Lord gave to me before I die. I asked the Lord to forgive me for every wrong that I have done. I believe that he did.

The blood of Jesus covers all sins, including disobedience and stubbornness. I wanted my own way, and I refused to obey the Lord, and the consequences resulted in the death of my husband and bad memories that my daughters will have to stand against in the Lord throughout their lifetimes. I apologize for all of the pain that I caused my daughters, and I pray that their souls, their minds are healed and recovered in the Lord Jesus Christ. For the Lord is a restorer of souls.

When we are forgiven by the Lord, old things, the old life, and hurtful memories are passed away if we stand in faith and cast down and remove everything negative memory, negative words spoken by people, and places that bring back negative memories. All of these thing will try to make us captive to our past. I refuse to be a captive anymore to my past. For the word of God says that God forgives me when I confess my sins to him. God cleanses me from all unrighteousness, and there is no condemnation in Christ Jesus. Therefore, *I refuse to walk in condemnation to please other people who want to see me suffer for what the Lord has already forgiven.* I choose to live in freedom in the Lord.

Freedom!

Freedom is a state of mind. It is the ability to feel that you are not chained to a thought, idea, event or people that limit your movement and your ability to go where you want to go and do what you want to do. The ultimate level of freedom is when you do not have to hide or worry about what someone thinks of you. I just want to be free. I want the freedom to tell my story and help others. I want my family to be able to move forward in life without the shackles of worry and limitation that people place on you when they find out "the secret." I want the cloud of obscurity to dissipate. If you have a secret, then there is always the threat of exposure. I want to eliminate that threat. So, here is my life, an open book.

APPENDIX

THE STRENGTH TO ENDURE

"Thy word is a lamp unto my feet, and a light unto my path."
(Psalm 119:105)

God's word will sustain you through any storm. His word will give you the strength and the power to live through anything and to emerge victorious in the end. God's word is a lamp unto our feet and light unto our paths. Below are scriptures that I meditated on day and night to help heal the pain and disappear the negative effects of the tragic event my family had to endure. These scriptures will help you stay in the fight and build a determination in you to win. They build a bridge of safety upon which to walk when life feels unstable. Most of all, they will give you the confidence to stand in the midst of the storm and reclaim your hope and trust in the midst of any adversity.

Hebrews 13:5-6

"Let your conversation be without covetousness; and be content with such things as ye have: for he hath said, I will never leave thee, nor forsake thee.

[6] So that we may boldly say, The Lord is my helper, and I will not fear what man shall do unto me."

Isaiah 46:4

"Even to your old age and gray hairs I am he, I am he who will sustain you. I have made you and I will carry you; I will sustain you and I will rescue you."

Isaiah 49:23

"...you will know that I am the Lord; those who hope in me will not be disappointed."

Jeremiah 9:24

"...but let him who boasts-boast about this that he understands and knows me, that I am the Lord, who exercises kindness, justice, and righteousness on earth, for in these I delight."

Psalm 34:5-6, 19

"They looked unto him and were lightened: and their faces were not ashamed. [6] This poor man cried, and the LORD heard him, and saved him out of all his troubles.

[19] Many are the afflictions of the righteous: but the LORD delivered him out of them all.

John 18:36

Jesus said, "My kingdom is not of this world ... but now my kingdom is from another place."

Luke 17:21

"...the kingdom of God is within you."

Romans 10:8-11

But what does it say? "The word is near you; it is in your mouth and in your heart," that is, the message concerning faith that we proclaim:

[9] If you declare with your mouth, "Jesus is Lord," and believe in your heart that God raised him from the dead, you will be saved.

[10] For it is with your heart that you believe and are justified, and it is with your mouth that you profess your faith and are saved.

[11] As Scripture says, "Anyone who believes in him will never be put to shame."

Philippians 3:20

"But our citizenship is in heaven..."

Ephesians 2:19

"You are no longer foreigners and aliens, but fellow citizens with God's people and members of God's household."

Ephesians 4:22-23

"You were taught with regard to your former way of life, to put off your old self, which is being corrupted by its deceitful desires; to be made new in the attitude of your minds; and to put on the new self, created to be like God in true righteousness and holiness."

Isaiah 43:18-19

"Forget the former things; do not dwell on the past. See, I am doing a new thing! Now it springs up; do you not perceive it? I am making a way in the desert and streams in the wasteland."

Isaiah 42:16

"I will lead the blind by ways they have not known, along unfamiliar paths. I will guide them; I will turn the darkness into light before them and make the rough places smooth. These are the things I will do; I will not forsake them."

Isaiah 41:10

"So do not fear, for I am with you; do not be dismayed, for I am you God. I will strengthen you and help you; I will uphold you with my righteous right hand."

Isaiah 50:4-5, 7

"The Sovereign Lord has given me an instructed tongue to know the word that sustains the weary. He wakens me morning by morning, wakens my ear to listen like one being taught. The Sovereign Lord has opened my ears, and I have not been rebellious; [7] because the Sovereign Lord helps me, I will not be disgraced. Therefore, have I set my face like flint, and I know I will not be put to shame."

Isaiah 54:17

"'No weapon forged against you will prevail, and you will refute every tongue that accuses you. This is the heritage of the servants of the Lord, and this is their vindication from me,' declares the Lord."

Proverbs 1:33

"But whoever listens to me will live in safety and be at ease, without fear of harm."

Proverbs 9:6, 10

"Leave your simple ways and you will live; walk in the way of insight."

^{10} *The fear of the LORD is the beginning of wisdom, and knowledge of the Holy One is understanding."*

Proverbs 12:4

"A wife of noble character is her husband's crown, but a disgraceful wife is like decay in his bones."

Proverbs 12:24

"Diligent hands will rule, but laziness ends in slave labor."

Proverbs 13:4

"The sluggard craves and gets nothing, but the desires of the diligent are fully satisfied."

Proverbs 15:32

"He who ignores discipline despises himself, but whoever heeds correction gains understanding."

Proverbs 16:2

"All a man's ways seem innocent to him, but motives are weighted by the Lord."

Proverbs 28:14, 26

[14] Blessed is the one who always trembles before God, but whoever hardens their heart falls into trouble.

[26] Those who trust in themselves are fools, but those who walk in wisdom are kept safe."

Joel 2:25

"I will repay you for the years the locusts have eaten—the great locust and the young locust, the other locusts and the locust swarm— my great army that I sent among you."

Joel 2:25 (Amplified)

"And I will restore or replace for you the years that the locust has eaten—the hopping locust, the stripping locust, and the crawling locust, My great army which I sent among you."

Ephesians 6:10

"Finally, be strong in the Lord and in his mighty power."

Acts 1:8

"But you will receive power when the Holy Spirit comes on you; and you will be my witnesses in Jerusalem, and in all Judea and Samaria, and to the ends of the earth."

Ephesians 6:11-12

"Put on the full armor of God, so that you can take your stand against the devil's schemes. [12] For our struggle is not against flesh and blood, but against the rulers, against the authorities, against the powers of this dark world and against the spiritual forces of evil in the heavenly realms."

I must have on God's whole armor so that I can successfully stand up against [all] the strategies and deceits of the devil.

In order to resist and stand my ground on the evil day [of danger], I must have on God's complete armor. God's whole armor makes or equips me to stand firm after I have done all the crises demands. I can stand firmly in my place—I can hold my ground.

Truth: I must know the truth as it is revealed in the word of God about the situation or circumstance.

Righteousness: I must know that I am made right with God. I have right standing with Him. He is for me.

Preparation: Being prepared, in a constant state of readiness (like a trained soldier), which comes from knowing the truth in the Gospel of peace.

Faith: a solid, firm unwavering trust in the word of God. I believe God instead of what my senses tell me.

Salvation: I must know that I have been saved from destruction.

Word of God: It is power in my mouth. When I speak it, the word of God causes change to occur in my life and things to line up with what I am saying. Power is released to cause circumstances and situations to line up with what I am saying about them which is what the word of God says about them, and God's word accomplishes what it sets out to do.

John 1:1-44

"In the beginning was the Word, and the Word was with God, and the Word was God.

[2] He was with God in the beginning.

[3] Through him all things were made; without him nothing was made that has been made.

[4] In him was life, and that life was the light of all mankind.

[5] The light shines in the darkness, and the darkness has not overcome it."

John 3:14-21

"Just as Moses lifted up the snake in the wilderness, so the Son of Man must be lifted up,

[15] that everyone who believes may have eternal life in him."

[16] For God so loved the world that he gave his one and only Son, that whoever believes in him shall not perish but have eternal life.

[17] For God did not send his Son into the world to condemn the world, but to save the world through him.

[18] Whoever believes in him is not condemned, but whoever does not believe stands condemned already because they have not believed in the name of God's one and only Son.

[19] This is the verdict: Light has come into the world, but people loved darkness instead of light because their deeds were evil.

[20] Everyone who does evil hates the light and will not come into the light for fear that their deeds will be exposed.

[21] But whoever lives by the truth comes into the light, so that it may be seen plainly that what they have done has been done in the sight of God."

John 4:21-24

"Woman," Jesus replied, "believe me, a time is coming when you will worship the Father neither on this mountain nor in Jerusalem.

[22] You Samaritans worship what you do not know; we worship what we do know, for salvation is from the Jews.

[23] Yet a time is coming and has now come when the true worshipers will worship the Father in the Spirit and in truth, for they are the kind of worshipers the Father seeks.

[24] God is spirit, and his worshipers must worship in the Spirit and in truth."

John 5:1-42

Sometime later, Jesus went up to Jerusalem for one of the Jewish festivals.

2 Now there is in Jerusalem near the Sheep Gate a pool, which in Aramaic is called Bethesda and which is surrounded by five covered colonnades.

3 Here a great number of disabled people used to lie—the blind, the lame, the paralyzed. [4]

5 One who was there had been an invalid for thirty-eight years.

6 When Jesus saw him lying there and learned that he had been in this condition for a long time, he asked him, "Do you want to get well?"

7 "Sir," the invalid replied, "I have no one to help me into the pool when the water is stirred. While I am trying to get in, someone else goes down ahead of me."

8 Then Jesus said to him, "Get up! Pick up your mat and walk."

9 At once the man was cured; he picked up his mat and walked. The day on which this took place was a Sabbath,

10 and so the Jewish leaders said to the man who had been healed, "It is the Sabbath; the law forbids you to carry your mat."

11 But he replied, "The man who made me well said to me, 'Pick up your mat and walk.'"

12 So they asked him, "Who is this fellow who told you to pick it up and walk?"

13 The man who was healed had no idea who it was, for Jesus had slipped away into the crowd that was there.

¹⁴ Later Jesus found him at the temple and said to him, "See, you are well again. Stop sinning or something worse may happen to you."

¹⁵ The man went away and told the Jewish leaders that it was Jesus who had made him well.

¹⁶ So, because Jesus was doing these things on the Sabbath, the Jewish leaders began to persecute him.

¹⁷ In his defense Jesus said to them, "My Father is always at his work to this very day, and I too am working."

¹⁸ For this reason they tried all the more to kill him; not only was he breaking the Sabbath, but he was even calling God his own Father, making himself equal with God.

¹⁹ Jesus gave them this answer: "Very truly I tell you, the Son can do nothing by himself; he can do only what he sees his Father doing, because whatever the Father does the Son also does.

²⁰ For the Father loves the Son and shows him all he does. Yes, and he will show him even greater works than these, so that you will be amazed.

²¹ For just as the Father raises the dead and gives them life, even so the Son gives life to whom he is pleased to give it.

²² Moreover, the Father judges no one, but has entrusted all judgment to the Son,

²³ that all may honor the Son just as they honor the Father. Whoever does not honor the Son does not honor the Father, who sent him.

²⁴ "Very truly I tell you, whoever hears my word and believes him who sent me has eternal life and will not be judged but has crossed over from death to life.

²⁵ Very truly I tell you, a time is coming and has now come when the dead will hear the voice of the Son of God and those who hear will live.

26 For as the Father has life in himself, so he has granted the Son also to have life in himself.

27 And he has given him authority to judge because he is the Son of Man.

35 Then Jesus declared, "I am the bread of life. Whoever comes to me will never go hungry, and whoever believes in me will never be thirsty.

36 But as I told you, you have seen me and still you do not believe.

37 All those the Father gives me will come to me, and whoever comes to me I will never drive away.

38 For I have come down from heaven not to do my will but to do the will of him who sent me.

39 And this is the will of him who sent me that I shall lose none of all those he has given me but raise them up at the last day.

40 For my Father's will is that everyone who looks to the Son and believes in him shall have eternal life, and I will raise them up at the last day."

41 At this the Jews there began to grumble about him because he said, "I am the bread that came down from heaven."

42 They said, "Is this not Jesus, the son of Joseph, whose father and mother we know? How can he now say, 'I came down from heaven'?"

43 "Stop grumbling among yourselves," Jesus answered.

44 "No one can come to me unless the Father who sent me draws them, and I will raise them up at the last day.

^{45} It is written in the Prophets: 'They will all be taught by God.' Everyone who has heard the Father and learned from him comes to me.

^{46} No one has seen the Father except the one who is from God; only he has seen the Father.

^{47} Very truly I tell you, the one who believes has eternal life.

^{48} I am the bread of life.

^{49} Your ancestors ate the manna in the wilderness, yet they died.

^{50} But here is the bread that comes down from heaven, which anyone may eat and not die.

^{51} I am the living bread that came down from heaven. Whoever eats this bread will live forever. This bread is my flesh, which I will give for the life of the world."

^{52} Then the Jews began to argue sharply among themselves, "How can this man give us his flesh to eat?"

^{53} Jesus said to them, "Very truly I tell you, unless you eat the flesh of the Son of Man and drink his blood, you have no life in you.

^{54} Whoever eats my flesh and drinks my blood has eternal life, and I will raise them up at the last day.

^{55} For my flesh is real food and my blood is real drink.

^{56} Whoever eats my flesh and drinks my blood remains in me, and I in them.

^{57} Just as the living Father sent me and I live because of the Father, so the one who feeds on me will live because of me.

^{58} This is the bread that came down from heaven. Your ancestors ate manna and died, but whoever feeds on this bread will live forever."

^{59} He said this while teaching in the synagogue in Capernaum.

[60] *On hearing it, many of his disciples said, "This is a hard teaching. Who can accept it?"*

[61] *Aware that his disciples were grumbling about this, Jesus said to them, "Does this offend you?*

[62] *Then what if you see the Son of Man ascend to where he was before!*

[63] *The Spirit gives life; the flesh counts for nothing. The words I have spoken to you—they are full of the Spirit[e] and life.*

[64] *Yet there are some of you who do not believe." For Jesus had known from the beginning which of them did not believe and who would betray him.*

[65] *He went on to say, "This is why I told you that no one can come to me unless the Father has enabled them."*

[66] *From this time many of his disciples turned back and no longer followed him.*

[67] *"You do not want to leave too, do you?" Jesus asked the Twelve.*

[68] *Simon Peter answered him, "Lord, to whom we shall go? You have the words of eternal life.*

[69] *We have come to believe and to know that you are the Holy One of God."*

[70] *Then Jesus replied, "Have I not chosen you, the Twelve? Yet one of you is a devil!"*

[71] *(He meant Judas, the son of Simon Iscariot, who, though one of the Twelve, was later to betray him.)*

John 8:4-18

And said to Jesus, "Teacher, this woman was caught in the act of adultery.

⁵ *In the Law Moses commanded us to stone such women. Now what do you say?"*

⁶ *They were using this question as a trap, in order to have a basis for accusing him. But Jesus bent down and started to write on the ground with his finger.*

⁷ *When they kept on questioning him, he straightened up and said to them, "Let any one of you who is without sin be the first to throw a stone at her."*

⁸ *Again he stooped down and wrote on the ground.*

⁹ *At this, those who heard began to go away one at a time, the older ones first, until only Jesus was left, with the woman still standing there.*

¹⁰ *Jesus straightened up and asked her, "Woman, where are they? Has no one condemned you?"*

¹¹ *"No one, sir," she said, "Then neither do I condemn you," Jesus declared. "Go now and leave your life of sin."*

¹² *When Jesus spoke again to the people, he said, "I am the light of the world. Whoever follows me will never walk in darkness but will have the light of life."*

¹³ *The Pharisees challenged him, "Here you are, appearing as your own witness; your testimony is not valid."*

¹⁴ *Jesus answered, "Even if I testify on my own behalf, my testimony is valid, for I know where I came from and where I am going. But you have no idea where I come from or where I am going.*

¹⁵ *You judge by human standards; I pass judgment on no one.*

¹⁶ *But if I do judge, my decisions are true, because I am not alone. I stand with the Father, who sent me.*

[17] In your own Law it is written that the testimony of two witnesses is true.

[18] I am one who testifies for myself; my other witness is the Father, who sent me."

John 12:20-32

Now there were some Greeks among those who went up to worship at the festival.

[21] They came to Philip, who was from Bethsaida in Galilee, with a request. "Sir," they said, "we would like to see Jesus."

[22] Philip went to tell Andrew; Andrew and Philip in turn told Jesus.

[23] Jesus replied, "The hour has come for the Son of Man to be glorified.

[24] Very truly I tell you, unless a kernel of wheat falls to the ground and dies, it remains only a single seed. But if it dies, it produces many seeds.

[25] Anyone who loves their life will lose it, while anyone who hates their life in this world will keep it for eternal life.

[26] Whoever serves me must follow me; and where I am, my servant also will be. My Father will honor the one who serves me.

[27] "Now my soul is troubled, and what shall I say? 'Father, save me from this hour'? No, it was for this very reason I came to this hour.

[28] Father, glorify your name!" Then a voice came from heaven, "I have glorified it, and will glorify it again."

[29] The crowd that was there heard it said it had thundered; others said an angel had spoken to him.

[30] Jesus said, "This voice was for your benefit, not mine.

³¹ Now is the time for judgment on this world; now the prince of this world will be driven out.

³² And I, when I am lifted up from the earth, will draw all people to myself."

John 9:1-17

As he went along, he saw a man blind from birth.

² His disciples asked him, "Rabbi, who sinned, this man or his parents, that he was born blind?"

³ "Neither this man nor his parents sinned," said Jesus, "but this happened so that the works of God might be displayed in him.

⁴ As long as it is day, we must do the works of him who sent me. Night is coming when no one can work.

⁵ While I am in the world, I am the light of the world."

⁶ After saying this, he spit on the ground, made some mud with the saliva, and put it on the man's eyes.

⁷ "Go," he told him, "wash in the Pool of Siloam" (this word means "Sent"). So, the man went and washed and came home seeing.

⁸ His neighbors and those who had formerly seen him begging asked, "Isn't this the same man who used to sit and beg?"

⁹ Some claimed that he was. Others said, "No, he only looks like him." But he himself insisted, "I am the man."

¹⁰ "How then were your eyes opened?" they asked.

¹¹ He replied, "The man they call Jesus made some mud and put it on my eyes. He told me to go to Siloam and wash. So I went and washed, and then I could see."

¹² "Where is this man?" they asked him. "I don't know," he said.

13 They brought to the Pharisees the man who had been blind.

14 Now the day on which Jesus had made the mud and opened the man's eyes was a Sabbath.

15 Therefore the Pharisees also asked him how he had received his sight. "He put mud on my eyes," the man replied, "and I washed, and now I see."

16 Some of the Pharisees said, "This man is not from God, for he does not keep the Sabbath." But others asked, "How can a sinner perform such signs?" So, they were divided.

17 Then they turned again to the blind man, "What have you to say about him? It was your eyes he opened."

John 9:35-41

Jesus heard that they had thrown him out, and when he found him, he said, "Do you believe in the Son of Man?"

36 "Who is he, sir?" the man asked. "Tell me so that I may believe in him."

37 Jesus said, "You have now seen him; in fact, he is the one speaking with you."

38 Then the man said, "Lord, I believe," and he worshiped him.

39 Jesus said, "For judgment I have come into this world, so that the blind will see and those who see will become blind."

40 Some Pharisees who were with him heard him say this and asked, "What? Are we blind too?"

41 Jesus said, "If you were blind, you would not be guilty of sin; but now that you claim you can see, your guilt remains.

John 11:20-53

When Martha heard that Jesus was coming, she went out to meet him, but Mary stayed at home.

[21] "Lord," Martha said to Jesus, "if you had been here, my brother would not have died.

[22] But I know that even now God will give you whatever you ask."

[23] Jesus said to her, "Your brother will rise again."

[24] Martha answered, "I know he will rise again in the resurrection at the last day."

[25] Jesus said to her, "I am the resurrection and the life. The one who believes in me will live, even though they die;

[26] and whoever lives by believing in me will never die. Do you believe this?"

[27] "Yes, Lord," she replied, "I believe that you are the Messiah, the Son of God, who is to come into the world."

[28] After she had said this, she went back and called her sister Mary aside. "The Teacher is here," she said, "and is asking for you."

[29] When Mary heard this, she got up quickly and went to him.

[30] Now Jesus had not yet entered the village but was still at the place where Martha had met him.

[31] When the Jews who had been with Mary in the house, comforting her, noticed how quickly she got up and went out, they followed her, supposing she was going to the tomb to mourn there.

[32] When Mary reached the place where Jesus was and saw him, she fell at his feet and said, "Lord, if you had been here, my brother would not have died."

[33] *When Jesus saw her weeping, and the Jews who had come along with her also weeping, he was deeply moved in spirit and troubled.*

[34] *"Where have you laid him?" he asked. "Come and see, Lord," they replied.*

[35] *Jesus wept.*

[36] *Then the Jews said, "See how he loved him!"*

[37] *But some of them said, "Could not he who opened the eyes of the blind man have kept this man from dying?"*

[38] *Jesus, once more deeply moved, came to the tomb. It was a cave with a stone laid across the entrance.*

[39] *"Take away the stone," he said. "But, Lord," said Martha, the sister of the dead man, "by this time there is a bad odor, for he has been there four days."*

[40] *Then Jesus said, "Did I not tell you that if you believe, you will see the glory of God?"*

[41] *So they took away the stone. Then Jesus looked up and said, "Father, I thank you that you have heard me.*

[42] *I knew that you always hear me, but I said this for the benefit of the people standing here, that they may believe that you sent me."*

[43] *When he had said this, Jesus called in a loud voice, "Lazarus, come out!"*

[44] *The dead man came out, his hands and feet wrapped with strips of linen, and a cloth around his face. Jesus said to them, "Take off the grave clothes and let him go."*

[45] *Therefore many of the Jews who had come to visit Mary, and had seen what Jesus did, believed in him.*

⁴⁶ But some of them went to the Pharisees and told them what Jesus had done.

⁴⁷ Then the chief priests and the Pharisees called a meeting of the Sanhedrin. "What are we accomplishing?" they asked. "Here is this man performing many signs.

⁴⁸ If we let him go on like this, everyone will believe in him, and then the Romans will come and take away both our temple and our nation."

⁴⁹ Then one of them, named Caiaphas, who was high priest that year, spoke up, "You know nothing at all!

⁵⁰ You do not realize that it is better for you that one man die for the people than that the whole nation perish."

⁵¹ He did not say this on his own, but as high priest that year he prophesied that Jesus would die for the Jewish nation,

⁵² and not only for that nation but also for the scattered children of God, to bring them together and make them one.

⁵³ So from that day on they plotted to take his life.

John 15:1-27

"I am the true vine, and my Father is the gardener.

² He cuts off every branch in me that bears no fruit, while every branch that does bear fruit, he prunes so that it will be even more fruitful.

³ You are already clean because of the word I have spoken to you.

⁴ Remain in me, as I also remain in you. No branch can bear fruit by itself; it must remain in the vine. Neither can you bear fruit unless you remain in me.

⁵ "I am the vine; you are the branches. If you remain in me and me in you, you will bear much fruit; apart from me you can do nothing.

⁶ If you do not remain in me, you are like a branch that is thrown away and withers; such branches are picked up, thrown into the fire and burned.

⁷ If you remain in me and my words remain in you, ask whatever you wish, and it will be done for you.

⁸ This is to my Father's glory, that you bear much fruit, showing yourselves to be my disciples.

⁹ "As the Father has loved me, so have I loved you. Now remain in my love.

¹⁰ If you keep my commands, you will remain in my love, just as I have kept my Father's commands and remain in his love.

¹¹ I have told you this so that my joy may be in you and that your joy may be complete.

¹² My command is this: Love each other as I have loved you.

¹³ Greater love has no one than this: to lay down one's life for one's friends.

¹⁴ You are my friends if you do what I command.

¹⁵ I no longer call you servants, because a servant does not know his master's business. Instead, I have called you friends, for everything that I learned from my Father I have made known to you.

¹⁶ You did not choose me, but I chose you and appointed you so that you might go and bear fruit—fruit that will last—and so that whatever you ask in my name the Father will give you.

¹⁷ This is my command: Love each other.

[18] *"If the world hates you, keep in mind that it hated me first.*

[19] *If you belonged to the world, it would love you as its own. As it is, you do not belong to the world, but I have chosen you out of the world. That is why the world hates you.*

[20] *Remember what I told you: 'A servant is not greater than his master.' If they persecuted me, they will persecute you also. If they obeyed my teaching, they will obey yours also.*

[21] *They will treat you this way because of my name, for they do not know the one who sent me.*

[22] *If I had not come and spoken to them, they would not be guilty of sin; but now they have no excuse for their sin.*

[23] *Whoever hates me hates my Father as well.*

[24] *If I had not done among them the works no one else did, they would not be guilty of sin. As it is, they have seen, and yet they have hated both me and my Father.*

[25] *But this is to fulfill what is written in their Law: 'They hated me without reason.'*

[26] *"When the Advocate comes, whom I will send to you from the Father—the Spirit of truth who goes out from the Father—he will testify about me.*

[27] *And you also must testify, for you have been with me from the beginning.*

Galatians 5:13-26

For, brethren, ye have been called unto liberty; only use not liberty for an occasion to the flesh, but by love serve one another.

[14] *For all the law is fulfilled in one word, even in this; Thou shalt love thy neighbor as thyself.*

^{15} But if ye bite and devour one another, take heed that ye be not consumed one of another.

^{16} This I say then, Walk in the Spirit, and ye shall not fulfil the lust of the flesh.

^{17} For the flesh lusted against the Spirit, and the Spirit against the flesh: and these are contrary the one to the other: so that ye cannot do the things that ye would.

^{18} But if ye be led of the Spirit, ye are not under the law.

^{19} Now the works of the flesh are manifest, which are these; Adultery, fornication, uncleanness, lasciviousness,

^{20} Idolatry, witchcraft, hatred, variance, emulations, wrath, strife, seditions, heresies,

^{21} Envying's, murders, drunkenness, reveling, and such like: of the which I tell you before, as I have also told you in time past, that they which do such things shall not inherit the kingdom of God.

^{22} But the fruit of the Spirit is love, joy, peace, longsuffering, gentleness, goodness, faith,

^{23} Meekness, temperance: against such there is no law.

^{24} And they that are Christ's have crucified the flesh with the affections and lusts.

^{25} If we live in the Spirit, let us also walk in the Spirit.

^{26} Let us not be desirous of vain glory, provoking one another, envying one another.

John 6:35-71

And Jesus said unto them, I am the bread of life: he that cometh to me shall never hunger; and he that believeth on me shall never thirst.

^{36} But I said unto you, That ye also have seen me, and believe not.

^{37} *All that the Father giveth me shall come to me; and him that cometh to me I will in no wise cast out.*

^{38} *For I came down from heaven, not to do mine own will, but the will of him that sent me.*

^{39} *And this is the Father's will which hath sent me, that of all which he hath given me I should lose nothing but should raise it up again at the last day.*

^{40} *And this is the will of him that sent me, that everyone which see the Son, and believeth on him, may have everlasting life: and I will raise him up at the last day.*

REFERENCES

Abel, G. (2001). *The Stop Child Molestation Book.* (p. 38). Xlibris Corporation. DOI: Retrieved from www.xlibris.co

Barbaree, H. E., Marshal, W. L., & Hudson, S. M. (1993). *The Juvenile Sex Offender,* 5-107. New York: Guilford Press.

In text citation: (Barbaree, Marshal & Hudson, 1993)

Galloway, S., & Houston, J. (2008). *Sexual Offending and Mental Health: Multidisciplinary Management in the Community*, 10-12. London: In Forensic Focus. London: Jessica Kingsley Publishers. DOI: *Sexual Offending and Mental Health: Multidisciplinary Management in the Community*

Child Sexual Abuse: What Parents Should Know, Retrieved from http://www.apa.org/pi/families/resources/child-sexual-abuse.aspx

Finkel, M. A., & Giardino, A. P. (2002). *Medical Evaluation Of Child Sexual Abuse A Practical Guide,* -10, 20-22. Thousand Oaks: Sage Publications, Inc.

ABOUT THE AUTHOR

Valencia Black

Valencia Black lives in San Bernardino County, California. She is a widow who was married 43 years but she was with her husband since she was in high school. They spent 49-years together in total. She raised five grown children: Four daughters and one son, who have families of their own. She has two small dogs with loving humanlike personalities that bring her joy and comfort. Valencia has known God from a little girl, but she received Christ Jesus as her Savior and Lord at age 22. She has walked with God for over forty-four years.

"Some say that history is written by the winners. However, there are times when the Lord allows the conquered to rewrite the lies and expose the truth."

Valencia Black

Made in the USA
Columbia, SC
14 December 2024

48177431R00065